ULTIMATE TRAINING PLANNER

Bibliografische Information der Deutschen Nationalbibliothek:
Die Deutsche Nationalbibliothek verzeichnet diese Publikation in der Deutschen
Nationalbibliografie; detaillierte bibliografische Daten sind im Internet über
http://dnb.dnb.de abrufbar.

© 2024 Niklas Siebenhüter
Verlag: BoD · Books on Demand GmbH, In de Tarpen 42, 22848 Norderstedt
Druck: Libri Plureos GmbH, Friedensallee 273, 22763 Hamburg
ISBN: 978-3-7597-9610-3

WORKOUT TRACKER

WORKOUT TRACKER

DATE

START TIME

END TIME

EXERCISE/ MUSCLES

BACK CHEST BICEPS TRICEPS FRONT DELTS REAR DELTS SIDE DELTS QUADS HAMSTRINGS GLUTES CALVES TRAPS ABS

CAD	S1	S2	S3	S4	S5	S6
WT / REPS / RIR		REST	REST	REST	REST	REST
WT / REPS / RIR		REST	REST	REST	REST	REST
WT / REPS / RIR		REST	REST	REST	REST	REST
WT / REPS / RIR		REST	REST	REST	REST	REST
WT / REPS / RIR		REST	REST	REST	REST	REST
WT / REPS / RIR		REST	REST	REST	REST	REST
WT / REPS / RIR		REST	REST	REST	REST	REST
WT / REPS / RIR		REST	REST	REST	REST	REST

CAD = Cadence
S = Set
WT = Weight
REPS = Repetitions
RIR = Repetitions in Reserve

WORKOUT TRACKER

EXERCISE/ MUSCLES		CAD	S1	S2	S3	S4	S5	S6
	WT							
	REPS			REST	REST	REST	REST	REST
	RIR							
	WT							
	REPS			REST	REST	REST	REST	REST
	RIR							
	WT							
	REPS			REST	REST	REST	REST	REST
	RIR							
	WT							
	REPS			REST	REST	REST	REST	REST
	RIR							
	WT							
	REPS			REST	REST	REST	REST	REST
	RIR							
	WT							
	REPS			REST	REST	REST	REST	REST
	RIR							
	WT							
	REPS			REST	REST	REST	REST	REST
	RIR							
	WT							
	REPS			REST	REST	REST	REST	REST
	RIR							

BACK CHEST BICEPS TRICEPS FRONT DELTS REAR DELTS SIDE DELTS QUADS HAMSTRINGS GLUTES CALVES TRAPS ABS

DATE

START TIME

END TIME

CAD = Cadence

S = Set

WT = Weight

REPS = Repetitions

RIR = Repetitions in reserve

WORKOUT TRACKER

DATE

START TIME

END TIME

CAD = Cadence

S = Set

WT = Weight

REPS = Repetitions

RIR = Repetitions in Reserve

EXERCISE/MUSCLES	CAD	S1	S2	S3	S4	S5	S6
	WT		REST	REST	REST	REST	REST
	REPS						
	RIR						
	WT		REST	REST	REST	REST	REST
	REPS						
	RIR						
	WT		REST	REST	REST	REST	REST
	REPS						
	RIR						
	WT		REST	REST	REST	REST	REST
	REPS						
	RIR						
	WT		REST	REST	REST	REST	REST
	REPS						
	RIR						
	WT		REST	REST	REST	REST	REST
	REPS						
	RIR						
	WT		REST	REST	REST	REST	REST
	REPS						
	RIR						

BACK CHEST BICEPS TRICEPS FRONT DELTS REAR DELTS SIDE DELTS QUADS HAMSTRINGS GLUTES CALVES TRAPS ABS

WORKOUT TRACKER

EXERCISE/ MUSCLES		S1	S2	S3	S4	S5	S6
	WT						
	REPS		REST	REST	REST	REST	REST
	RIR						
	WT						
	REPS		REST	REST	REST	REST	REST
	RIR						
	WT						
	REPS		REST	REST	REST	REST	REST
	RIR						
	WT						
	REPS		REST	REST	REST	REST	REST
	RIR						
	WT						
	REPS		REST	REST	REST	REST	REST
	RIR						
	WT						
	REPS		REST	REST	REST	REST	REST
	RIR						
	WT						
	REPS		REST	REST	REST	REST	REST
	RIR						
	CAD						

BACK CHEST BICEPS TRICEPS FRONT DELTS REAR DELTS SIDE DELTS QUADS HAMSTRINGS GLUTES CALVES TRAPS ABS

DATE

START TIME

END TIME

CAD = Cadence

S = Set

WT = Weight

REPS = Repetitions

RIR = Repetitions In Reserve

WORKOUT TRACKER

EXERCISE/ MUSCLES		CAD		S1	S2	S3	S4	S5	S6
		WT							
		REPS			REST	REST	REST	REST	REST
		RIR							
		WT							
		REPS			REST	REST	REST	REST	REST
		RIR							
		WT							
		REPS			REST	REST	REST	REST	REST
		RIR							
		WT							
		REPS			REST	REST	REST	REST	REST
		RIR							
		WT							
		REPS			REST	REST	REST	REST	REST
		RIR							
		WT							
		REPS			REST	REST	REST	REST	REST
		RIR							
		WT							
		REPS			REST	REST	REST	REST	REST
		RIR							
		WT							
		REPS			REST	REST	REST	REST	REST
		RIR							

BACK CHEST BICEPS TRICEPS FRONT DELTS REAR DELTS SIDE DELTS QUADS HAMSTRINGS GLUTES CALVES TRAPS ABS

DATE

START TIME

END TIME

CAD = Cadence

S = Set

WT = Weight

REPS = Repetitions

RIR = Repetitions In Reserve

WORKOUT TRACKER

EXERCISE/ MUSCLES

BACK CHEST BICEPS TRICEPS FRONT DELTS REAR DELTS SIDE DELTS QUADS HAMSTRINGS GLUTES CALVES TRAPS ABS

DATE

START TIME   END TIME

CAD = Cadence

S = Set   **WT** = Weight

REPS = Repetitions   **RIR** = Repetitions in reserve

	CAD	S1	S2	S3	S4	S5	S6
WT REPS RIR			REST	REST	REST	REST	REST
WT REPS RIR			REST	REST	REST	REST	REST
WT REPS RIR			REST	REST	REST	REST	REST
WT REPS RIR			REST	REST	REST	REST	REST
WT REPS RIR			REST	REST	REST	REST	REST
WT REPS RIR			REST	REST	REST	REST	REST
WT REPS RIR			REST	REST	REST	REST	REST

WORKOUT TRACKER

EXERCISE/ MUSCLES

BACK · CHEST · BICEPS · TRICEPS · FRONT DELTS · REAR DELTS · SIDE DELTS · QUADS · HAMSTRINGS · GLUTES · CALVES · TRAPS · ABS

DATE

START TIME

END TIME

CAD = Cadence
S = Set
WT = Weight
REPS = Repetitions
RIR = Repetitions In reserve

	CAD	S1	S2	S3	S4	S5	S6
WT			REST	REST	REST	REST	REST
REPS							
RIR							
WT			REST	REST	REST	REST	REST
REPS							
RIR							
WT			REST	REST	REST	REST	REST
REPS							
RIR							
WT			REST	REST	REST	REST	REST
REPS							
RIR							
WT			REST	REST	REST	REST	REST
REPS							
RIR							
WT			REST	REST	REST	REST	REST
REPS							
RIR							
WT			REST	REST	REST	REST	REST
REPS							
RIR							
WT			REST	REST	REST	REST	REST
REPS							
RIR							

WORKOUT TRACKER

DATE

START TIME

END TIME

CAD = Cadence
S = Set
WT = Weight

REPS = Repetitions
RIR = Repetitions in reserve

BACK CHEST BICEPS TRICEPS FRONT DELTS REAR DELTS SIDE DELTS QUADS HAMSTRINGS GLUTES CALVES TRAPS ABS

EXERCISE/ MUSCLES	CAD	S1	S2	S3	S4	S5	S6
	WT						
	REPS						
	RIR						
	WT						
	REPS						
	RIR						
	WT						
	REPS						
	RIR						
	WT						
	REPS						
	RIR						
	WT						
	REPS						
	RIR						
	WT						
	REPS						
	RIR						
	WT						
	REPS						
	RIR						
	WT						
	REPS						
	RIR						
	WT						
	REPS						
	RIR						
	WT						
	REPS						
	RIR						

REST REST REST REST REST

WORKOUT TRACKER

EXERCISE/ MUSCLES

BACK CHEST BICEPS TRICEPS FRONT DELTS REAR DELTS SIDE DELTS QUADS HAMSTRINGS GLUTES CALVES TRAPS ABS

DATE

START TIME

END TIME

CAD	S1	S2	S3	S4	S5	S6
REPS						
WT						
RIR	REST	REST	REST	REST	REST	

CAD = Cadence

S = Set

WT = Weight

REPS = Repetitions

RIR = Repetitions In Reserve

WORKOUT TRACKER

DATE

START TIME

END TIME

CAD = Cadence

REPS = Repetitions

S = Set

WT = Weight

RIR = Repetitions In reserve

EXERCISE/ MUSCLES		CAD		S1	S2	S3	S4	S5	S6
BACK CHEST BICEPS TRICEPS FRONT DELTS REAR DELTS SIDE DELTS QUADS HAMSTRINGS GLUTES CALVES TRAPS ABS			WT						
			REPS						
			RIR	REST	REST	REST	REST	REST	REST
			WT						
			REPS						
			RIR	REST	REST	REST	REST	REST	REST
			WT						
			REPS						
			RIR	REST	REST	REST	REST	REST	REST
			WT						
			REPS						
			RIR	REST	REST	REST	REST	REST	REST
			WT						
			REPS						
			RIR	REST	REST	REST	REST	REST	REST
			WT						
			REPS						
			RIR	REST	REST	REST	REST	REST	REST
			WT						
			REPS						
			RIR	REST	REST	REST	REST	REST	REST

WORKOUT TRACKER

EXERCISE/MUSCLES

BACK CHEST BICEPS TRICEPS FRONT DELTS REAR DELTS SIDE DELTS QUADS HAMSTRINGS GLUTES CALVES TRAPS ABS

DATE

START TIME

END TIME

	CAD	S1	S2	S3	S4	S5	S6
WT / REPS / RIR			REST	REST	REST	REST	REST
WT / REPS / RIR			REST	REST	REST	REST	REST
WT / REPS / RIR			REST	REST	REST	REST	REST
WT / REPS / RIR			REST	REST	REST	REST	REST
WT / REPS / RIR			REST	REST	REST	REST	REST
WT / REPS / RIR			REST	REST	REST	REST	REST
WT / REPS / RIR			REST	REST	REST	REST	REST
WT / REPS / RIR			REST	REST	REST	REST	REST
WT / REPS / RIR			REST	REST	REST	REST	REST
WT / REPS / RIR			REST	REST	REST	REST	REST

CAD = Cadence **REPS** = Repetitions

S = Set **RIR** = Repetitions in reserve

WT = Weight

WORKOUT TRACKER

DATE

BACK CHEST BICEPS TRICEPS FRONT DELTS REAR DELTS SIDE DELTS QUADS HAMSTRINGS GLUTES CALVES TRAPS ABS

START TIME

END TIME

EXERCISE/ MUSCLES	CAD		S1	S2	S3	S4	S5	S6
		WT						
		REPS	REST	REST	REST	REST	REST	REST
		RIR						
		WT						
		REPS	REST	REST	REST	REST	REST	REST
		RIR						
		WT						
		REPS	REST	REST	REST	REST	REST	REST
		RIR						
		WT						
		REPS	REST	REST	REST	REST	REST	REST
		RIR						
		WT						
		REPS	REST	REST	REST	REST	REST	REST
		RIR						
		WT						
		REPS	REST	REST	REST	REST	REST	REST
		RIR						
		WT						
		REPS	REST	REST	REST	REST	REST	REST
		RIR						
		WT						
		REPS	REST	REST	REST	REST	REST	REST
		RIR						

CAD = Cadence

S = Set

WT = Weight

REPS = Repetitions

RIR = Repetitions In Reserve

© ULTIMATE TRAINING PLANNER

WORKOUT TRACKER

EXERCISE/ MUSCLES

BACK CHEST BICEPS TRICEPS FRONT DELTS REAR DELTS SIDE DELTS QUADS HAMSTRINGS GLUTES CALVES TRAPS ABS

DATE

START TIME

END TIME

	CAD	S1	S2	S3	S4	S5	S6
WT / REPS / RIR			REST	REST	REST	REST	REST
WT / REPS / RIR			REST	REST	REST	REST	REST
WT / REPS / RIR			REST	REST	REST	REST	REST
WT / REPS / RIR			REST	REST	REST	REST	REST
WT / REPS / RIR			REST	REST	REST	REST	REST
WT / REPS / RIR			REST	REST	REST	REST	REST
WT / REPS / RIR			REST	REST	REST	REST	REST
WT / REPS / RIR			REST	REST	REST	REST	REST
WT / REPS / RIR			REST	REST	REST	REST	REST
WT / REPS / RIR			REST	REST	REST	REST	REST
WT / REPS / RIR			REST	REST	REST	REST	REST

CAD = Cadence
S = Set
WT = Weight
REPS = Repetitions
RIR = Repetitions in reserve

WORKOUT TRACKER

DATE

START TIME

END TIME

EXERCISE/MUSCLES — BACK CHEST BICEPS TRICEPS FRONT DELTS REAR DELTS SIDE DELTS QUADS HAMSTRINGS GLUTES CALVES TRAPS ABS

CAD = Cadence

S = Set

WT = Weight

REPS = Repetitions

RIR = Repetitions In Reserve

EXERCISE/MUSCLES	CAD		S1	S2	S3	S4	S5	S6
		WT						
		REPS						
		RIR						
		WT						
		REPS						
		RIR						
		WT						
		REPS						
		RIR						
		WT						
		REPS						
		RIR						
		WT						
		REPS						
		RIR						
		WT						
		REPS						
		RIR						
		WT						
		REPS						
		RIR						
		WT						
		REPS						
		RIR						
		WT						
		REPS						
		RIR						
		WT						
		REPS						
		RIR						

REST ... REST ... REST ... REST ... REST

WORKOUT TRACKER

DATE

START TIME

END TIME

CAD = Cadence
S = Set
WT = Weight

REPS = Repetitions
RIR = Repetitions in Reserve

EXERCISE/ MUSCLES	CAD	S1	S2	S3	S4	S5	S6
	WT						
	REPS						
	RIR	REST	REST	REST	REST	REST	
	WT						
	REPS						
	RIR	REST	REST	REST	REST	REST	
	WT						
	REPS						
	RIR	REST	REST	REST	REST	REST	
	WT						
	REPS						
	RIR	REST	REST	REST	REST	REST	
	WT						
	REPS						
	RIR	REST	REST	REST	REST	REST	
	WT						
	REPS						
	RIR	REST	REST	REST	REST	REST	
	WT						
	REPS						
	RIR	REST	REST	REST	REST	REST	

BACK CHEST BICEPS TRICEPS FRONT DELTS REAR DELTS SIDE DELTS QUADS HAMSTRINGS GLUTES CALVES TRAPS ABS

WORKOUT TRACKER

DATE

START TIME

END TIME

CAD = Cadence

S = Set

WT = Weight

REPS = Repetitions

RIR = Repetitions in reserve

EXERCISE/ MUSCLES

BACK CHEST BICEPS TRICEPS FRONT DELTS REAR DELTS SIDE DELTS QUADS HAMSTRINGS GLUTES CALVES TRAPS ABS

	CAD	S1	S2	S3	S4	S5	S6
WT							
REPS							
RIR							
WT							
REPS							
RIR							
WT							
REPS							
RIR							
WT							
REPS							
RIR							
WT							
REPS							
RIR							
WT							
REPS							
RIR							
WT							
REPS							
RIR							
WT							
REPS							
RIR							
WT							
REPS							
RIR							
WT							
REPS							
RIR							

REST REST REST REST REST

WORKOUT TRACKER

DATE

START TIME

END TIME

CAD = Cadence   **REPS** = Repetitions

S = Set   **RIR** = Repetitions in Reserve

WT = Weight

EXERCISE/MUSCLES	BACK CHEST BICEPS TRICEPS FRONT DELTS REAR DELTS SIDE DELTS QUADS HAMSTRINGS GLUTES CALVES TRAPS ABS	CAD	S1	S2	S3	S4	S5	S6

Column sub-headers per exercise row: WT / REPS / RIR

REST

WORKOUT TRACKER

EXERCISE/ MUSCLES

BACK CHEST BICEPS TRICEPS FRONT DELTS REAR DELTS SIDE DELTS QUADS HAMSTRINGS GLUTES CALVES TRAPS ABS

DATE

START TIME
END TIME

CAD = Cadence
S = Set
WT = Weight

REPS = Repetitions
RIR = Repetitions in reserve

CAD		S1	S2	S3	S4	S5	S6
	WT						
	REPS						
	RIR	REST	REST	REST	REST	REST	REST
	WT						
	REPS						
	RIR	REST	REST	REST	REST	REST	REST
	WT						
	REPS						
	RIR	REST	REST	REST	REST	REST	REST
	WT						
	REPS						
	RIR	REST	REST	REST	REST	REST	REST
	WT						
	REPS						
	RIR	REST	REST	REST	REST	REST	REST
	WT						
	REPS						
	RIR	REST	REST	REST	REST	REST	REST
	WT						
	REPS						
	RIR	REST	REST	REST	REST	REST	REST
	WT						
	REPS						
	RIR	REST	REST	REST	REST	REST	REST

WORKOUT TRACKER

DATE

START TIME

END TIME

CAD = Cadence   **REPS** = Repetitions

S = Set   **RIR** = Repetitions in Reserve

WT = Weight

EXERCISE/ MUSCLES	CAD	S1		S2		S3		S4		S5		S6
	WT REPS RIR		REST		REST		REST		REST		REST	
	WT REPS RIR		REST		REST		REST		REST		REST	
	WT REPS RIR		REST		REST		REST		REST		REST	
	WT REPS RIR		REST		REST		REST		REST		REST	
	WT REPS RIR		REST		REST		REST		REST		REST	
	WT REPS RIR		REST		REST		REST		REST		REST	

BACK CHEST BICEPS TRICEPS FRONT DELTS REAR DELTS SIDE DELTS QUADS HAMSTRINGS GLUTES CALVES TRAPS ABS

WORKOUT TRACKER

DATE

START TIME

END TIME

BACK CHEST BICEPS TRICEPS FRONT DELTS REAR DELTS SIDE DELTS QUADS HAMSTRINGS GLUTES CALVES TRAPS ABS

CAD = Cadence
S = Set
WT = Weight
REPS = Repetitions
RIR = Repetitions in reserve

EXERCISE/MUSCLES	CAD	S1	S2	S3	S4	S5	S6
	WT						
	REPS						
	RIR						
	WT						
	REPS						
	RIR						
	WT						
	REPS						
	RIR						
	WT						
	REPS						
	RIR						
	WT						
	REPS						
	RIR						
	WT						
	REPS						
	RIR						
	WT						
	REPS						
	RIR						
	WT						
	REPS						
	RIR						
	WT						
	REPS						
	RIR						
	WT						
	REPS						
	RIR						

WORKOUT TRACKER

EXERCISE/
MUSCLES

BACK CHEST BICEPS TRICEPS FRONT DELTS REAR DELTS SIDE DELTS QUADS HAMSTRINGS GLUTES CALVES TRAPS ABS

DATE

START TIME

END TIME

	CAD	S1	S2	S3	S4	S5	S6
WT			REST	REST	REST	REST	REST
REPS							
RIR							

CAD = Cadence

S = Set

WT = Weight

REPS = Repetitions

RIR = Repetitions In Reserve

WORKOUT TRACKER

DATE

START TIME

END TIME

EXERCISE/ MUSCLES

BACK CHEST BICEPS TRICEPS FRONT DELTS REAR DELTS SIDE DELTS QUADS HAMSTRINGS GLUTES CALVES TRAPS ABS

CAD = Cadence

S = Set

WT = Weight

REPS = Repetitions

RIR = Repetitions In Reserve

EXERCISE/MUSCLES	CAD		S1	S2	S3	S4	S5	S6
		WT						
		REPS						
		RIR						
		WT						
		REPS						
		RIR						
		WT						
		REPS						
		RIR						
		WT						
		REPS						
		RIR						
		WT						
		REPS						
		RIR						
		WT						
		REPS						
		RIR						
		WT						
		REPS						
		RIR						

REST

WORKOUT TRACKER

EXERCISE/ MUSCLES		CAD	S1	S2	S3	S4	S5	S6
	WT							
	REPS							
	RIR			REST	REST	REST	REST	REST
	WT							
	REPS							
	RIR			REST	REST	REST	REST	REST
	WT							
	REPS							
	RIR			REST	REST	REST	REST	REST
	WT							
	REPS							
	RIR			REST	REST	REST	REST	REST
	WT							
	REPS							
	RIR			REST	REST	REST	REST	REST
	WT							
	REPS							
	RIR			REST	REST	REST	REST	REST
	WT							
	REPS							
	RIR			REST	REST	REST	REST	REST
	WT							
	REPS							
	RIR			REST	REST	REST	REST	REST

BACK CHEST BICEPS TRICEPS FRONT DELTS REAR DELTS SIDE DELTS QUADS HAMSTRINGS GLUTES CALVES TRAPS ABS

DATE

START TIME

END TIME

CAD = Cadence
S = Set
WT = Weight
REPS = Repetitions
RIR = Repetitions In Reserve

© ULTIMATE TRAINING PLANNER

WORKOUT TRACKER

EXERCISE/ MUSCLES

BACK CHEST BICEPS TRICEPS FRONT DELTS REAR DELTS SIDE DELTS QUADS HAMSTRINGS GLUTES CALVES TRAPS ABS

DATE

START TIME

END TIME

CAD = Cadence

S = Set

WT = Weight

REPS = Repetitions

RIR = Repetitions In Reserve

CAD	S1	S2	S3	S4	S5	S6
WT						
REPS						
RIR	REST	REST	REST	REST	REST	REST
WT						
REPS						
RIR	REST	REST	REST	REST	REST	REST
WT						
REPS						
RIR	REST	REST	REST	REST	REST	REST
WT						
REPS						
RIR	REST	REST	REST	REST	REST	REST
WT						
REPS						
RIR	REST	REST	REST	REST	REST	REST
WT						
REPS						
RIR	REST	REST	REST	REST	REST	REST
WT						
REPS						
RIR	REST	REST	REST	REST	REST	REST
WT						
REPS						
RIR	REST	REST	REST	REST	REST	REST
WT						
REPS						
RIR	REST	REST	REST	REST	REST	REST
WT						
REPS						
RIR	REST	REST	REST	REST	REST	REST

WORKOUT TRACKER

EXERCISE/ MUSCLES

BACK CHEST BICEPS TRICEPS FRONT DELTS REAR DELTS SIDE DELTS QUADS HAMSTRINGS GLUTES CALVES TRAPS ABS

DATE

START TIME

END TIME

	CAD	S1	S2	S3	S4	S5	S6
WT							
REPS							
RIR			REST	REST	REST	REST	REST

CAD = Cadence
S = Set
WT = Weight
REPS = Repetitions
RIR = Repetitions in reserve

WORKOUT TRACKER

DATE

START TIME

END TIME

CAD = Cadence

S = Set

WT = Weight

REPS = Repetitions

RIR = Repetitions in reserve

EXERCISE/ MUSCLES	CAD		S1	S2	S3	S4	S5	S6
	WT							
	REPS							
	RIR		REST	REST	REST	REST	REST	
	WT							
	REPS							
	RIR		REST	REST	REST	REST	REST	
	WT							
	REPS							
	RIR		REST	REST	REST	REST	REST	
	WT							
	REPS							
	RIR		REST	REST	REST	REST	REST	
	WT							
	REPS							
	RIR		REST	REST	REST	REST	REST	
	WT							
	REPS							
	RIR		REST	REST	REST	REST	REST	
	WT							
	REPS							
	RIR		REST	REST	REST	REST	REST	

BACK CHEST BICEPS TRICEPS FRONT DELTS REAR DELTS SIDE DELTS QUADS HAMSTRINGS GLUTES CALVES TRAPS ABS

© ULTIMATE TRAINING PLANNER

WORKOUT TRACKER

DATE

START TIME

END TIME

EXERCISE/ MUSCLES

BACK CHEST BICEPS TRICEPS FRONT DELTS REAR DELTS SIDE DELTS QUADS HAMSTRINGS GLUTES CALVES TRAPS ABS

	CAD	S1	S2	S3	S4	S5	S6
WT / RIR / REPS			REST	REST	REST	REST	REST

CAD = Cadence   **REPS** = Repetitions

S = Set   **RIR** = Repetitions In Reserve

WT = Weight

© ULTIMATE **TRAINING** PLANNER

WORKOUT TRACKER

DATE

START TIME

END TIME

EXERCISE/ MUSCLES	CAD		S1		S2		S3		S4		S5		S6
		WT											
		REPS		REST		REST		REST		REST		REST	
		RIR											
		WT											
		REPS		REST		REST		REST		REST		REST	
		RIR											
		WT											
		REPS		REST		REST		REST		REST		REST	
		RIR											
		WT											
		REPS		REST		REST		REST		REST		REST	
		RIR											
		WT											
		REPS		REST		REST		REST		REST		REST	
		RIR											
		WT											
		REPS		REST		REST		REST		REST		REST	
		RIR											
		WT											
		REPS		REST		REST		REST		REST		REST	
		RIR											

BACK   CHEST   BICEPS   TRICEPS   FRONT DELTS   REAR DELTS   SIDE DELTS   QUADS   HAMSTRINGS   GLUTES   CALVES   TRAPS   ABS

CAD = Cadence

S = Set

WT = Weight

REPS = Repetitions

RIR = Repetitions in reserve

© ULTIMATE **TRAINING** PLANNER

WORKOUT TRACKER

EXERCISE/ MUSCLES	DATE												
	CAD	S1			S2			S3			S4		

BACK CHEST BICEPS TRICEPS FRONT DELTS REAR DELTS SIDE DELTS QUADS HAMSTRINGS GLUTES CALVES TRAPS ABS

DATE

START TIME

END TIME

CAD = Cadence
S = Set
WT = Weight
REPS = Repetitions
RIR = Repetitions In Reserve

WT
REPS
RIR

REST

S1 S2 S3 S4 S5 S6

© ULTIMATE **TRAINING** PLANNER

WORKOUT TRACKER

DATE

START TIME

END TIME

EXERCISE/ MUSCLES	CAD	S1		S2		S3		S4		S5		S6
	WT											
	REPS											
	RIR											
	WT											
	REPS											
	RIR											
	WT											
	REPS											
	RIR											
	WT											
	REPS											
	RIR											
	WT											
	REPS											
	RIR											
	WT											
	REPS											
	RIR											
	WT											
	REPS											
	RIR											

BACK CHEST BICEPS TRICEPS FRONT DELTS REAR DELTS SIDE DELTS QUADS HAMSTRINGS GLUTES CALVES TRAPS ABS

REST

CAD = Cadence

S = Set

WT = Weight

REPS = Repetitions

RIR = Repetitions in reserve

© ULTIMATE **TRAINING** PLANNER

WORKOUT TRACKER

DATE

START TIME

END TIME

CAD = Cadence
REPS = Repetitions
S = Set
RIR = Repetitions In Reserve
WT = Weight

EXERCISE/ MUSCLES	CAD	S1	S2	S3	S4	S5	S6
BACK CHEST BICEPS TRICEPS FRONT DELTS REAR DELTS SIDE DELTS QUADS HAMSTRINGS GLUTES CALVES TRAPS ABS	WT REPS RIR		REST	REST	REST	REST	REST

WORKOUT TRACKER

EXERCISE/MUSCLES			CAD	S1	S2	S3	S4	S5	S6
		WT							
		REPS							
		RIR							
		WT							
		REPS							
		RIR							
		WT							
		REPS							
		RIR							
		WT							
		REPS							
		RIR							
		WT							
		REPS							
		RIR							
		WT							
		REPS							
		RIR							
		WT							
		REPS							
		RIR							
		WT							
		REPS							
		RIR							

BACK CHEST BICEPS TRICEPS FRONT DELTS REAR DELTS SIDE DELTS QUADS HAMSTRINGS GLUTES CALVES TRAPS ABS

DATE

START TIME

END TIME

CAD = Cadence
S = Set
WT = Weight

REPS = Repetitions
RIR = Repetitions In Reserve

© ULTIMATE **TRAINING** PLANNER

WORKOUT TRACKER

DATE

START TIME

END TIME

CAD = Cadence REPS = Repetitions

S = Set RIR = Repetitions In Reserve

WT = Weight

EXERCISE/MUSCLES	BACK CHEST BICEPS TRICEPS FRONT DELTS REAR DELTS SIDE DELTS QUADS HAMSTRINGS GLUTES CALVES TRAPS ABS	CAD		S1	S2	S3	S4	S5	S6
		WT			REST	REST	REST	REST	REST
		REPS							
		RIR							
		WT			REST	REST	REST	REST	REST
		REPS							
		RIR							
		WT			REST	REST	REST	REST	REST
		REPS							
		RIR							
		WT			REST	REST	REST	REST	REST
		REPS							
		RIR							
		WT			REST	REST	REST	REST	REST
		REPS							
		RIR							
		WT			REST	REST	REST	REST	REST
		REPS							
		RIR							

WORKOUT TRACKER

DATE

START TIME

END TIME

CAD = Cadence   **REPS** = Repetitions

S = Set   **RIR** = Repetitions in reserve

WT = Weight

EXERCISE/ MUSCLES	CAD		S1	S2	S3	S4	S5	S6
BACK		WT						
		REPS						
		RIR						
CHEST		WT						
		REPS						
		RIR						
BICEPS		WT						
		REPS						
		RIR						
TRICEPS		WT						
		REPS						
		RIR						
FRONT DELTS		WT						
		REPS						
		RIR						
REAR DELTS		WT						
		REPS						
		RIR						
SIDE DELTS		WT						
		REPS						
		RIR						
QUADS		WT						
		REPS						
		RIR						
HAMSTRINGS		WT						
		REPS						
		RIR						
GLUTES		WT						
		REPS						
		RIR						
CALVES		WT						
		REPS						
		RIR						
TRAPS		WT						
		REPS						
		RIR						
ABS		WT						
		REPS						
		RIR						

WORKOUT TRACKER

EXERCISE/ MUSCLES

BACK CHEST BICEPS TRICEPS FRONT DELTS REAR DELTS SIDE DELTS QUADS HAMSTRINGS GLUTES CALVES TRAPS ABS

DATE

START TIME

END TIME

	CAD	S1	S2	S3	S4	S5	S6
WT / REPS / RIR			REST	REST	REST	REST	REST
WT / REPS / RIR			REST	REST	REST	REST	REST
WT / REPS / RIR			REST	REST	REST	REST	REST
WT / REPS / RIR			REST	REST	REST	REST	REST
WT / REPS / RIR			REST	REST	REST	REST	REST
WT / REPS / RIR			REST	REST	REST	REST	REST
WT / REPS / RIR			REST	REST	REST	REST	REST
WT / REPS / RIR			REST	REST	REST	REST	REST
WT / REPS / RIR			REST	REST	REST	REST	REST
WT / REPS / RIR			REST	REST	REST	REST	REST
WT / REPS / RIR			REST	REST	REST	REST	REST

CAD = Cadence

S = Set

WT = Weight

REPS = Repetitions

RIR = Repetitions in reserve

WORKOUT TRACKER

EXERCISE/ MUSCLES

BACK CHEST BICEPS TRICEPS FRONT DELTS REAR DELTS SIDE DELTS QUADS HAMSTRINGS GLUTES CALVES TRAPS ABS

DATE

START TIME

END TIME

	CAD	S1	S2	S3	S4	S5	S6
WT							
REPS							
RIR							

CAD = Cadence
S = Set
WT = Weight
REPS = Repetitions
RIR = Repetitions In Reserve

REST

© ULTIMATE **TRAINING** PLANNER

WORKOUT TRACKER

EXERCISE/ MUSCLES

BACK CHEST BICEPS TRICEPS FRONT DELTS REAR DELTS SIDE DELTS QUADS HAMSTRINGS GLUTES CALVES TRAPS ABS

DATE

START TIME

END TIME

CAD = Cadence

S = Set

WT = Weight

REPS = Repetitions

RIR = Repetitions In Reserve

CAD	S1	S2	S3	S4	S5	S6

WT / REPS / RIR

REST

WORKOUT TRACKER

EXERCISE/ MUSCLES

BACK CHEST BICEPS TRICEPS FRONT DELTS REAR DELTS SIDE DELTS QUADS HAMSTRINGS GLUTES CALVES TRAPS ABS

DATE

START TIME   END TIME

	CAD	S1	S2	S3	S4	S5	S6
WT / REPS / RIR			REST	REST	REST	REST	REST

CAD = Cadence
REPS = Repetitions
S = Set
RIR = Repetitions in Reserve
WT = Weight

WORKOUT TRACKER

EXERCISE/ MUSCLES

BACK CHEST BICEPS TRICEPS FRONT DELTS REAR DELTS SIDE DELTS QUADS HAMSTRINGS GLUTES CALVES TRAPS ABS

DATE

START TIME

END TIME

CAD	S1	S2	S3	S4	S5	S6

WT REPS RIR

REST

CAD = Cadence
S = Set
WT = Weight
REPS = Repetitions
RIR = Repetitions In reserve

WORKOUT TRACKER

EXERCISE/ MUSCLES

BACK CHEST BICEPS TRICEPS FRONT DELTS REAR DELTS SIDE DELTS QUADS HAMSTRINGS GLUTES CALVES TRAPS ABS

DATE

START TIME

END TIME

	CAD	S1	S2	S3	S4	S5	S6
WT / REPS / RIR			REST	REST	REST	REST	REST
WT / REPS / RIR			REST	REST	REST	REST	REST
WT / REPS / RIR			REST	REST	REST	REST	REST
WT / REPS / RIR			REST	REST	REST	REST	REST
WT / REPS / RIR			REST	REST	REST	REST	REST
WT / REPS / RIR			REST	REST	REST	REST	REST
WT / REPS / RIR			REST	REST	REST	REST	REST
WT / REPS / RIR			REST	REST	REST	REST	REST

CAD = Cadence **REPS** = Repetitions

S = Set

WT = Weight **RIR** = Repetitions In Reserve

WORKOUT TRACKER

DATE

START TIME

END TIME

CAD = Cadence **REPS** = Repetitions
S = Set **RIR** = Repetitions In
WT = Weight Reserve

EXERCISE/ MUSCLES	CAD		S1	S2	S3	S4	S5	S6
BACK CHEST BICEPS TRICEPS FRONT DELTS REAR DELTS SIDE DELTS QUADS HAMSTRINGS GLUTES CALVES TRAPS ABS		WT						
		REPS						
		RIR	REST	REST	REST	REST	REST	REST
		WT						
		REPS						
		RIR	REST	REST	REST	REST	REST	REST
		WT						
		REPS						
		RIR	REST	REST	REST	REST	REST	REST
		WT						
		REPS						
		RIR	REST	REST	REST	REST	REST	REST
		WT						
		REPS						
		RIR	REST	REST	REST	REST	REST	REST
		WT						
		REPS						
		RIR	REST	REST	REST	REST	REST	REST
		WT						
		REPS						
		RIR	REST	REST	REST	REST	REST	REST

WORKOUT TRACKER

DATE

START TIME | END TIME

CAD = Cadence   **REPS** = Repetitions
S = Set   **RIR** = Repetitions in Reserve
WT = Weight

EXERCISE/MUSCLES

BACK   CHEST   BICEPS   TRICEPS   FRONT DELTS   REAR DELTS   SIDE DELTS   QUADS   HAMSTRINGS   GLUTES   CALVES   TRAPS   ABS

	CAD	S1	S2	S3	S4	S5	S6
WT / REPS / RIR			REST	REST	REST	REST	REST
WT / REPS / RIR			REST	REST	REST	REST	REST
WT / REPS / RIR			REST	REST	REST	REST	REST
WT / REPS / RIR			REST	REST	REST	REST	REST
WT / REPS / RIR			REST	REST	REST	REST	REST
WT / REPS / RIR			REST	REST	REST	REST	REST
WT / REPS / RIR			REST	REST	REST	REST	REST
WT / REPS / RIR			REST	REST	REST	REST	REST
WT / REPS / RIR			REST	REST	REST	REST	REST
WT / REPS / RIR			REST	REST	REST	REST	REST

WORKOUT TRACKER

EXERCISE/ MUSCLES

BACK CHEST BICEPS TRICEPS FRONT DELTS REAR DELTS SIDE DELTS QUADS HAMSTRINGS GLUTES CALVES TRAPS ABS

DATE

START TIME

END TIME

CAD = Cadence

S = Set

WT = Weight

REPS = Repetitions

RIR = Repetitions in reserve

CAD	S1	S2	S3	S4	S5	S6
WT / REPS / RIR	REST	REST	REST	REST	REST	

WORKOUT TRACKER

EXERCISE/ MUSCLES

BACK CHEST BICEPS TRICEPS FRONT DELTS REAR DELTS SIDE DELTS QUADS HAMSTRINGS GLUTES CALVES TRAPS ABS

DATE

START TIME

END TIME

CAD	S1	S2	S3	S4	S5	S6
WT						
REPS						
RIR						

CAD = Cadence

S = Set

WT = Weight

REPS = Repetitions

RIR = Repetitions in reserve

REST

© ULTIMATE **TRAINING** PLANNER

WORKOUT TRACKER

DATE

START TIME

END TIME

CAD = Cadence	REPS = Repetitions
S = Set	RIR = Repetitions In
WT = Weight	reserve

EXERCISE/MUSCLES

BACK CHEST BICEPS TRICEPS FRONT DELTS REAR DELTS SIDE DELTS QUADS HAMSTRINGS GLUTES CALVES TRAPS ABS

CAD	S1	S2	S3	S4	S5	S6
REPS						
WT						
RIR	REST	REST	REST	REST	REST	

WORKOUT TRACKER

DATE

START TIME

END TIME

EXERCISE/ MUSCLES

BACK CHEST BICEPS TRICEPS FRONT DELTS REAR DELTS SIDE DELTS QUADS HAMSTRINGS GLUTES CALVES TRAPS ABS

EXERCISE/MUSCLES	CAD		S1	S2	S3	S4	S5	S6
	CAD	WT						
		REPS						
		RIR						
	CAD	WT						
		REPS						
		RIR						
	CAD	WT						
		REPS						
		RIR						
	CAD	WT						
		REPS						
		RIR						
	CAD	WT						
		REPS						
		RIR						
	CAD	WT						
		REPS						
		RIR						
	CAD	WT						
		REPS						
		RIR						
	CAD	WT						
		REPS						
		RIR						
	CAD	WT						
		REPS						
		RIR						
	CAD	WT						
		REPS						
		RIR						

REST

CAD = Cadence **REPS** = Repetitions
S = Set **RIR** = Repetitions in Reserve
WT = Weight

WORKOUT TRACKER

DATE

START TIME

END TIME

EXERCISE/ MUSCLES

BACK CHEST BICEPS TRICEPS FRONT DELTS REAR DELTS SIDE DELTS QUADS HAMSTRINGS GLUTES CALVES TRAPS ABS

CAD — Cadence
S = Set
WT = Weight
REPS = Repetitions
RIR = Repetitions In Reserve

CAD	S1	S2	S3	S4	S5	S6
WT / REPS / RIR	REST	REST	REST	REST	REST	
WT / REPS / RIR	REST	REST	REST	REST	REST	
WT / REPS / RIR	REST	REST	REST	REST	REST	
WT / REPS / RIR	REST	REST	REST	REST	REST	
WT / REPS / RIR	REST	REST	REST	REST	REST	
WT / REPS / RIR	REST	REST	REST	REST	REST	
WT / REPS / RIR	REST	REST	REST	REST	REST	
WT / REPS / RIR	REST	REST	REST	REST	REST	
WT / REPS / RIR	REST	REST	REST	REST	REST	
WT / REPS / RIR	REST	REST	REST	REST	REST	

WORKOUT TRACKER

© ULTIMATE **TRAINING** PLANNER.

DATE

START TIME

END TIME

CAD = Cadence   **REPS** = Repetitions

S = Set   **RIR** = Repetitions in reserve

WT = Weight

BACK CHEST BICEPS TRICEPS FRONT DELTS REAR DELTS SIDE DELTS QUADS HAMSTRINGS GLUTES CALVES TRAPS ABS

EXERCISE/ MUSCLES	CAD	S1	S2	S3	S4	S5	S6
	WT						
	REPS						
	RIR						
	WT						
	REPS						
	RIR						
	WT						
	REPS						
	RIR						
	WT						
	REPS						
	RIR						
	WT						
	REPS						
	RIR						
	WT						
	REPS						
	RIR						
	WT						
	REPS						
	RIR						
	WT						
	REPS						
	RIR						
	WT						
	REPS						
	RIR						
	WT						
	REPS						
	RIR						

WORKOUT TRACKER

EXERCISE/ MUSCLES

BACK CHEST BICEPS TRICEPS FRONT DELTS REAR DELTS SIDE DELTS QUADS HAMSTRINGS GLUTES CALVES TRAPS ABS

EXERCISE/MUSCLES	CAD			S1			S2			S3			S4			S5			S6
		RIR	REPS	WT	RIR	REPS	WT	RIR	REPS	WT	RIR	REPS	WT	RIR	REPS	WT	RIR	REPS	WT
						REST			REST			REST			REST			REST	
						REST			REST			REST			REST			REST	
						REST			REST			REST			REST			REST	
						REST			REST			REST			REST			REST	
						REST			REST			REST			REST			REST	
						REST			REST			REST			REST			REST	
						REST			REST			REST			REST			REST	

CAD = Cadence **REPS** = Repetitions
S = Set **RIR** = Repetitions in reserve
WT = Weight

WORKOUT TRACKER

START TIME

END TIME

CAD = Cadence

S = Set

WT = Weight

REPS = Repetitions

RIR = Repetitions in reserve

EXERCISE/ MUSCLES

BACK CHEST BICEPS TRICEPS FRONT DELTS REAR DELTS SIDE DELTS QUADS HAMSTRINGS GLUTES CALVES TRAPS ABS

CAD	S1	S2	S3	S4	S5	S6
WT REPS RIR						
WT REPS RIR						
WT REPS RIR						
WT REPS RIR						
WT REPS RIR						
WT REPS RIR						
WT REPS RIR						
WT REPS RIR						
WT REPS RIR						
WT REPS RIR						
WT REPS RIR						
WT REPS RIR						
WT REPS RIR						

WORKOUT TRACKER

EXERCISE/ MUSCLES

BACK CHEST BICEPS TRICEPS FRONT DELTS REAR DELTS SIDE DELTS QUADS HAMSTRINGS GLUTES CALVES TRAPS ABS

DATE

START TIME

END TIME

	CAD	S1	S2	S3	S4	S5	S6
WT / REPS / RIR			REST	REST	REST	REST	REST
WT / REPS / RIR			REST	REST	REST	REST	REST
WT / REPS / RIR			REST	REST	REST	REST	REST
WT / REPS / RIR			REST	REST	REST	REST	REST
WT / REPS / RIR			REST	REST	REST	REST	REST
WT / REPS / RIR			REST	REST	REST	REST	REST
WT / REPS / RIR			REST	REST	REST	REST	REST
WT / REPS / RIR			REST	REST	REST	REST	REST
WT / REPS / RIR			REST	REST	REST	REST	REST
WT / REPS / RIR			REST	REST	REST	REST	REST
WT / REPS / RIR			REST	REST	REST	REST	REST
WT / REPS / RIR			REST	REST	REST	REST	REST

CAD = Cadence

S = Set

WT = Weight

REPS = Repetitions

RIR = Repetitions In reserve

WORKOUT TRACKER

EXERCISE/ MUSCLES		CAD	S1	S2	S3	S4	S5	S6
	WT							
	REPS			REST	REST	REST	REST	REST
	RIR							
	WT							
	REPS			REST	REST	REST	REST	REST
	RIR							
	WT							
	REPS			REST	REST	REST	REST	REST
	RIR							
	WT							
	REPS			REST	REST	REST	REST	REST
	RIR							
	WT							
	REPS			REST	REST	REST	REST	REST
	RIR							
	WT							
	REPS			REST	REST	REST	REST	REST
	RIR							
	WT							
	REPS			REST	REST	REST	REST	REST
	RIR							
	WT							
	REPS			REST	REST	REST	REST	REST
	RIR							
	WT							
	REPS			REST	REST	REST	REST	REST
	RIR							

BACK CHEST BICEPS TRICEPS FRONT DELTS REAR DELTS SIDE DELTS QUADS HAMSTRINGS GLUTES CALVES TRAPS ABS

DATE

START TIME

END TIME

CAD = Cadence

S = Set

WT = Weight

REPS = Repetitions

RIR = Repetitions in Reserve

WORKOUT TRACKER

EXERCISE/ MUSCLES

BACK CHEST BICEPS TRICEPS FRONT DELTS REAR DELTS SIDE DELTS QUADS HAMSTRINGS GLUTES CALVES TRAPS ABS

DATE

START TIME

END TIME

	CAD	S1	S2	S3	S4	S5	S6
WT							
REPS							
RIR		REST	REST	REST	REST	REST	

CAD = Cadence **REPS** = Repetitions

S = Set **RIR** = Repetitions In Reserve

WT = Weight

© ULTIMATE **TRAINING** PLANNER

WORKOUT TRACKER

EXERCISE/ MUSCLES

BACK CHEST BICEPS TRICEPS FRONT DELTS REAR DELTS SIDE DELTS QUADS HAMSTRINGS GLUTES CALVES TRAPS ABS

DATE

START TIME
END TIME

CAD	S1	S2	S3	S4	S5	S6
WT / REPS / RIR		REST	REST	REST	REST	REST

CAD = Cadence
S = Set
WT = Weight
REPS = Repetitions
RIR = Repetitions in reserve

WORKOUT TRACKER

EXERCISE/ MUSCLES	CAD		S1		S2		S3		S4		S5		S6
		WT											
		REPS		REST		REST		REST		REST		REST	
		RIR											
		WT											
		REPS		REST		REST		REST		REST		REST	
		RIR											
		WT											
		REPS		REST		REST		REST		REST		REST	
		RIR											
		WT											
		REPS		REST		REST		REST		REST		REST	
		RIR											
		WT											
		REPS		REST		REST		REST		REST		REST	
		RIR											
		WT											
		REPS		REST		REST		REST		REST		REST	
		RIR											
		WT											
		REPS		REST		REST		REST		REST		REST	
		RIR											
		WT											
		REPS		REST		REST		REST		REST		REST	
		RIR											

BACK CHEST BICEPS TRICEPS FRONT DELTS REAR DELTS SIDE DELTS QUADS HAMSTRINGS GLUTES CALVES TRAPS ABS

DATE

START TIME

END TIME

CAD = Cadence

S = Set

WT = Weight

REPS = Repetitions

RIR = Repetitions in reserve

WORKOUT TRACKER

EXERCISE/ MUSCLES

BACK CHEST BICEPS TRICEPS FRONT DELTS REAR DELTS SIDE DELTS QUADS HAMSTRINGS GLUTES CALVES TRAPS ABS

DATE

START TIME

END TIME

	CAD	S1	S2	S3	S4	S5	S6
WT							
REPS							
RIR			REST	REST	REST	REST	REST

CAD = Cadence

S = Set

WT = Weight

REPS = Repetitions

RIR = Repetitions in Reserve

© ULTIMATE **TRAINING** PLANNER

WORKOUT TRACKER

EXERCISE/ MUSCLES		CAD	S1	S2	S3	S4	S5	S6
	REPS							
	WT		REST	REST	REST	REST	REST
	RIR							
	REPS							
	WT		REST	REST	REST	REST	REST
	RIR							
	REPS							
	WT		REST	REST	REST	REST	REST
	RIR							
	REPS							
	WT		REST	REST	REST	REST	REST
	RIR							
	REPS							
	WT		REST	REST	REST	REST	REST
	RIR							
	REPS							
	WT		REST	REST	REST	REST	REST
	RIR							
	REPS							
	WT		REST	REST	REST	REST	REST
	RIR							

BACK CHEST BICEPS TRICEPS FRONT DELTS REAR DELTS SIDE DELTS QUADS HAMSTRINGS GLUTES CALVES TRAPS ABS

DATE

START TIME

END TIME

CAD = Cadence

S = Set

WT = Weight

REPS = Repetitions

RIR = Repetitions in reserve

WORKOUT TRACKER

DATE

START TIME

END TIME

CAD = Cadence

S = Set

WT = Weight

REPS = Repetitions

RIR = Repetitions In reserve

EXERCISE/MUSCLES		CAD	S1	S2	S3	S4	S5	S6
BACK CHEST BICEPS TRICEPS FRONT DELTS REAR DELTS SIDE DELTS QUADS HAMSTRINGS GLUTES CALVES TRAPS ABS	WT REPS RIR			REST	REST	REST	REST	REST

WORKOUT TRACKER

DATE

START TIME

END TIME

EXERCISE/ MUSCLES

BACK CHEST BICEPS TRICEPS FRONT DELTS REAR DELTS SIDE DELTS QUADS HAMSTRINGS GLUTES CALVES TRAPS ABS

CAD	S1	S2	S3	S4	S5	S6

WT
REPS
RIR
REST

CAD = Cadence
S = Set
WT = Weight
REPS = Repetitions
RIR = Repetitions in reserve

WORKOUT TRACKER

EXERCISE/ MUSCLES

BACK CHEST BICEPS TRICEPS FRONT DELTS REAR DELTS SIDE DELTS QUADS HAMSTRINGS GLUTES CALVES TRAPS ABS

DATE

START TIME   END TIME

CAD = Cadence
REPS = Repetitions
S = Set
RIR = Repetitions in reserve
WT = Weight

CAD	S1	S2	S3	S4	S5	S6
WT / REPS / RIR						
WT / REPS / RIR						
WT / REPS / RIR						
WT / REPS / RIR						
WT / REPS / RIR						
WT / REPS / RIR						
WT / REPS / RIR						
WT / REPS / RIR						
WT / REPS / RIR						
WT / REPS / RIR						
WT / REPS / RIR						
WT / REPS / RIR						
WT / REPS / RIR						

REST ... REST ... REST ... REST ... REST

WORKOUT TRACKER

EXERCISE/ MUSCLES

BACK CHEST BICEPS TRICEPS FRONT DELTS REAR DELTS SIDE DELTS QUADS HAMSTRINGS GLUTES CALVES TRAPS ABS

DATE

START TIME

END TIME

CAD

CAD	S1	S2	S3	S4	S5	S6
WT / REPS / RIR		REST	REST	REST	REST	REST

CAD = Cadence
S = Set
WT = Weight
REPS = Repetitions
RIR = Repetitions in reserve

WORKOUT TRACKER

DATE

START TIME   END TIME

CAD = Cadence   **REPS** = Repetitions

S = Set   **RIR** = Repetitions in Reserve

WT = Weight

EXERCISE/ MUSCLES	CAD		S1	S2	S3	S4	S5	S6
		WT						
		REPS						
		RIR						
		WT						
		REPS						
		RIR						
		WT						
		REPS						
		RIR						
		WT						
		REPS						
		RIR						
		WT						
		REPS						
		RIR						
		WT						
		REPS						
		RIR						
		WT						
		REPS						
		RIR						
		WT						
		REPS						
		RIR						
		WT						
		REPS						
		RIR						

BACK CHEST BICEPS TRICEPS FRONT DELTS REAR DELTS SIDE DELTS QUADS HAMSTRINGS GLUTES CALVES TRAPS ABS

WORKOUT TRACKER

DATE

START TIME

END TIME

CAD = Cadence   **REPS** = Repetitions

S = Set   **RIR** = Repetitions In Reserve

WT = Weight

EXERCISE/MUSCLES	BACK CHEST BICEPS TRICEPS FRONT DELTS REAR DELTS SIDE DELTS QUADS HAMSTRINGS GLUTES CALVES TRAPS ABS	CAD		S1	S2	S3	S4	S5	S6
		WT							
		REPS			REST	REST	REST	REST	REST
		RIR							
		WT							
		REPS			REST	REST	REST	REST	REST
		RIR							
		WT							
		REPS			REST	REST	REST	REST	REST
		RIR							
		WT							
		REPS			REST	REST	REST	REST	REST
		RIR							
		WT							
		REPS			REST	REST	REST	REST	REST
		RIR							
		WT							
		REPS			REST	REST	REST	REST	REST
		RIR							

WORKOUT TRACKER

DATE

START TIME

END TIME

CAD = Cadence	REPS = Repetitions
S = Set	RIR = Repetitions in
WT = Weight	Reserve

BACK CHEST BICEPS TRICEPS FRONT DELTS REAR DELTS SIDE DELTS QUADS HAMSTRINGS GLUTES CALVES TRAPS ABS

EXERCISE/ MUSCLES	CAD		S1	S2	S3	S4	S5	S6
	WT							
	REPS							
	RIR							
	WT							
	REPS							
	RIR							
	WT							
	REPS							
	RIR							
	WT							
	REPS							
	RIR							
	WT							
	REPS							
	RIR							
	WT							
	REPS							
	RIR							
	WT							
	REPS							
	RIR							
	WT							
	REPS							
	RIR							
	WT							
	REPS							
	RIR							

WORKOUT TRACKER

EXERCISE/ MUSCLES

DATE

START TIME

END TIME

BACK CHEST BICEPS TRICEPS FRONT DELTS REAR DELTS SIDE DELTS QUADS HAMSTRINGS GLUTES CALVES TRAPS ABS

	CAD	S1	S2	S3	S4	S5	S6
WT REPS RIR			REST	REST	REST	REST	REST
WT REPS RIR			REST	REST	REST	REST	REST
WT REPS RIR			REST	REST	REST	REST	REST
WT REPS RIR			REST	REST	REST	REST	REST
WT REPS RIR			REST	REST	REST	REST	REST
WT REPS RIR			REST	REST	REST	REST	REST
WT REPS RIR			REST	REST	REST	REST	REST
WT REPS RIR			REST	REST	REST	REST	REST

CAD = Cadence

S = Set

WT = Weight

REPS = Repetitions

RIR = Repetitions In Reserve

WORKOUT TRACKER

DATE [ ]

CAD = Cadence   **REPS** = Repetitions
S = Set   **RIR** = Repetitions in reserve
WT = Weight

EXERCISE/ MUSCLES

BACK · CHEST · BICEPS · TRICEPS · FRONT DELTS · REAR DELTS · SIDE DELTS · QUADS · HAMSTRINGS · GLUTES · CALVES · TRAPS · ABS

EXERCISE/MUSCLES	CAD	S1	S2	S3	S4	S5	S6
		WT					
		REPS					
		RIR					
		REST	REST	REST	REST	REST	REST
		WT					
		REPS					
		RIR					
		REST	REST	REST	REST	REST	REST
		WT					
		REPS					
		RIR					
		REST	REST	REST	REST	REST	REST
		WT					
		REPS					
		RIR					
		REST	REST	REST	REST	REST	REST
		WT					
		REPS					
		RIR					
		REST	REST	REST	REST	REST	REST

WORKOUT TRACKER

EXERCISE/ MUSCLES

BACK CHEST BICEPS TRICEPS FRONT DELTS REAR DELTS SIDE DELTS QUADS HAMSTRINGS GLUTES CALVES TRAPS ABS

DATE

START TIME

END TIME

CAD = Cadence

S = Set

WT = Weight

REPS = Repetitions

RIR = Repetitions in reserve

CAD	S1	S2	S3	S4	S5	S6
WT / REPS / RIR		REST	REST	REST	REST	REST

REST

WORKOUT TRACKER

EXERCISE/ MUSCLES

BACK CHEST BICEPS TRICEPS FRONT DELTS REAR DELTS SIDE DELTS QUADS HAMSTRINGS GLUTES CALVES TRAPS ABS

DATE

START TIME
END TIME

CAD = Cadence
S = Set
WT = Weight

REPS = Repetitions
RIR = Repetitions in reserve

	CAD	S1	S2	S3	S4	S5	S6
WT REPS RIR							
WT REPS RIR							
WT REPS RIR							
WT REPS RIR							
WT REPS RIR							
WT REPS RIR							
WT REPS RIR							
WT REPS RIR							
WT REPS RIR							
WT REPS RIR							

REST

WORKOUT TRACKER

EXERCISE/ MUSCLES

BACK CHEST BICEPS TRICEPS FRONT DELTS REAR DELTS SIDE DELTS QUADS HAMSTRINGS GLUTES CALVES TRAPS ABS

DATE

START TIME

END TIME

	CAD	S1	S2	S3	S4	S5	S6
WT / RIR / REPS		REST	REST	REST	REST	REST	REST
WT / RIR / REPS		REST	REST	REST	REST	REST	REST
WT / RIR / REPS		REST	REST	REST	REST	REST	REST
WT / RIR / REPS		REST	REST	REST	REST	REST	REST
WT / RIR / REPS		REST	REST	REST	REST	REST	REST
WT / RIR / REPS		REST	REST	REST	REST	REST	REST
WT / RIR / REPS		REST	REST	REST	REST	REST	REST
WT / RIR / REPS		REST	REST	REST	REST	REST	REST
WT / RIR / REPS		REST	REST	REST	REST	REST	REST
WT / RIR / REPS		REST	REST	REST	REST	REST	REST
WT / RIR / REPS		REST	REST	REST	REST	REST	REST
WT / RIR / REPS		REST	REST	REST	REST	REST	REST

CAD = Cadence
S = Set
WT = Weight
REPS = Repetitions
RIR = Repetitions in reserve

WORKOUT TRACKER

DATE

START TIME

END TIME

CAD = Cadence   **REPS** = Repetitions

S = Set   **RIR** = Repetitions in Reserve

WT = Weight

EXERCISE/ MUSCLES	CAD	S1	S2	S3	S4	S5	S6
	WT REPS RIR		REST	REST	REST	REST	REST
	WT REPS RIR		REST	REST	REST	REST	REST
	WT REPS RIR		REST	REST	REST	REST	REST
	WT REPS RIR		REST	REST	REST	REST	REST
	WT REPS RIR		REST	REST	REST	REST	REST
	WT REPS RIR		REST	REST	REST	REST	REST
	WT REPS RIR		REST	REST	REST	REST	REST
	WT REPS RIR		REST	REST	REST	REST	REST
	WT REPS RIR		REST	REST	REST	REST	REST

BACK CHEST BICEPS TRICEPS FRONT DELTS REAR DELTS SIDE DELTS QUADS HAMSTRINGS GLUTES CALVES TRAPS ABS

WORKOUT TRACKER

EXERCISE/ MUSCLES	CAD		S1		S2		S3		S4		S5		S6
	WT												
	REPS			REST		REST		REST		REST		REST	
	RIR												
	WT												
	REPS			REST		REST		REST		REST		REST	
	RIR												
	WT												
	REPS			REST		REST		REST		REST		REST	
	RIR												
	WT												
	REPS			REST		REST		REST		REST		REST	
	RIR												
	WT												
	REPS			REST		REST		REST		REST		REST	
	RIR												
	WT												
	REPS			REST		REST		REST		REST		REST	
	RIR												

BACK CHEST BICEPS TRICEPS FRONT DELTS REAR DELTS SIDE DELTS QUADS HAMSTRINGS GLUTES CALVES TRAPS ABS

DATE

START TIME

END TIME

CAD = Cadence
S = Set
WT = Weight
REPS = Repetitions
RIR = Repetitions In Reserve

WORKOUT TRACKER

DATE

START TIME

END TIME

CAD = Cadence **REPS** = Repetitions
S = Set **RIR** = Repetitions in reserve
WT = Weight

EXERCISE/ MUSCLES	CAD	S1	S2	S3	S4	S5	S6
	WT						
	REPS						
	RIR						
	WT						
	REPS						
	RIR						
	WT						
	REPS						
	RIR						
	WT						
	REPS						
	RIR						
	WT						
	REPS						
	RIR						
	WT						
	REPS						
	RIR						
	WT						
	REPS						
	RIR						
	WT						
	REPS						
	RIR						

BACK CHEST BICEPS TRICEPS FRONT DELTS REAR DELTS SIDE DELTS QUADS HAMSTRINGS GLUTES CALVES TRAPS ABS

REST

WORKOUT TRACKER

EXERCISE/
MUSCLES

BACK CHEST BICEPS TRICEPS FRONT DELTS REAR DELTS SIDE DELTS QUADS HAMSTRINGS GLUTES CALVES TRAPS ABS

DATE

START TIME

END TIME

	CAD	S1	S2	S3	S4	S5	S6
WT			REST	REST	REST	REST	REST
REPS							
RIR							

CAD = Cadence

S = Set

WT = Weight

REPS = Repetitions

RIR = Repetitions in reserve

© ULTIMATE **TRAINING** PLANNER

WORKOUT TRACKER

DATE

START TIME   END TIME

CAD = Cadence   **REPS** = Repetitions
S = Set   **RIR** = Repetitions in reserve
WT = Weight

EXERCISE/ MUSCLES

BACK CHEST BICEPS TRICEPS FRONT DELTS REAR DELTS SIDE DELTS QUADS HAMSTRINGS GLUTES CALVES TRAPS ABS

EXERCISE/MUSCLES	CAD	S1	S2	S3	S4	S5	S6
	WT						
	REPS						
	RIR						
	WT						
	REPS						
	RIR						
	WT						
	REPS						
	RIR						
	WT						
	REPS						
	RIR						
	WT						
	REPS						
	RIR						
	WT						
	REPS						
	RIR						
	WT						
	REPS						
	RIR						
	WT						
	REPS						
	RIR						

WORKOUT TRACKER

EXERCISE/ MUSCLES

DATE

START TIME

END TIME

BACK CHEST BICEPS TRICEPS FRONT DELTS REAR DELTS SIDE DELTS QUADS HAMSTRINGS GLUTES CALVES TRAPS ABS

CAD = Cadence
S = Set
WT = Weight
REPS = Repetitions
RIR = Repetitions In Reserve

	CAD	S1	S2	S3	S4	S5	S6
WT							
REPS							
RIR		REST	REST	REST	REST	REST	REST
WT							
REPS							
RIR		REST	REST	REST	REST	REST	REST
WT							
REPS							
RIR		REST	REST	REST	REST	REST	REST
WT							
REPS							
RIR		REST	REST	REST	REST	REST	REST
WT							
REPS							
RIR		REST	REST	REST	REST	REST	REST
WT							
REPS							
RIR		REST	REST	REST	REST	REST	REST
WT							
REPS							
RIR		REST	REST	REST	REST	REST	REST

WORKOUT TRACKER

DATE

START TIME

END TIME

CAD = Cadence   **REPS** = Repetitions

S = Set   **RIR** = Repetitions in

WT = Weight   reserve

EXERCISE/ MUSCLES

BACK CHEST BICEPS TRICEPS FRONT DELTS REAR DELTS SIDE DELTS QUADS HAMSTRINGS GLUTES CALVES TRAPS ABS

CAD	S1	S2	S3	S4	S5	S6
WT REPS RIR						
WT REPS RIR						
WT REPS RIR						
WT REPS RIR						
WT REPS RIR						
WT REPS RIR						
WT REPS RIR						
WT REPS RIR						
WT REPS RIR						
WT REPS RIR						

WORKOUT TRACKER

EXERCISE/ MUSCLES

BACK CHEST BICEPS TRICEPS FRONT DELTS REAR DELTS SIDE DELTS QUADS HAMSTRINGS GLUTES CALVES TRAPS ABS

DATE

START TIME

END TIME

	CAD	S1	S2	S3	S4	S5	S6
WT			REST	REST	REST	REST	REST
REPS							
RIR							

CAD = Cadence REPS = Repetitions

S = Set RIR = Repetitions In reserve

WT = Weight

REST

© ULTIMATE **TRAINING** PLANNER.

WORKOUT TRACKER

DATE

START TIME

END TIME

CAD = Cadence   **REPS** = Repetitions
S = Set
WT = Weight
RIR = Repetitions in reserve

EXERCISE/ MUSCLES

BACK CHEST BICEPS TRICEPS FRONT DELTS REAR DELTS SIDE DELTS QUADS HAMSTRINGS GLUTES CALVES TRAPS ABS

CAD	S1	S2	S3	S4	S5	S6
WT / REPS / RIR		REST	REST	REST	REST	REST
WT / REPS / RIR		REST	REST	REST	REST	REST
WT / REPS / RIR		REST	REST	REST	REST	REST
WT / REPS / RIR		REST	REST	REST	REST	REST
WT / REPS / RIR		REST	REST	REST	REST	REST
WT / REPS / RIR		REST	REST	REST	REST	REST
WT / REPS / RIR		REST	REST	REST	REST	REST
WT / REPS / RIR		REST	REST	REST	REST	REST

WORKOUT TRACKER

DATE

START TIME

END TIME

CAD = Cadence

S = Set

WT = Weight

REPS = Repetitions

RIR = Repetitions in reserve

EXERCISE/MUSCLES	CAD		S1	S2	S3	S4	S5	S6
		WT						
		REPS						
		RIR	REST	REST	REST	REST	REST	REST

BACK CHEST BICEPS TRICEPS FRONT DELTS REAR DELTS SIDE DELTS QUADS HAMSTRINGS GLUTES CALVES TRAPS ABS

© ULTIMATE **TRAINING** PLANNER

WORKOUT TRACKER

DATE

START TIME END TIME

EXERCISE/MUSCLES

BACK CHEST BICEPS TRICEPS FRONT DELTS REAR DELTS SIDE DELTS QUADS HAMSTRINGS GLUTES CALVES TRAPS ABS

CAD = Cadence **REPS** = Repetitions
S = Set **RIR** = Repetitions in reserve
WT = Weight

EXERCISE/ MUSCLES	CAD	S1	S2	S3	S4	S5	S6
	WT						
	REPS		REST	REST	REST	REST	REST
	RIR						
	WT						
	REPS		REST	REST	REST	REST	REST
	RIR						
	WT						
	REPS		REST	REST	REST	REST	REST
	RIR						
	WT						
	REPS		REST	REST	REST	REST	REST
	RIR						
	WT						
	REPS		REST	REST	REST	REST	REST
	RIR						
	WT						
	REPS		REST	REST	REST	REST	REST
	RIR						
	WT						
	REPS		REST	REST	REST	REST	REST
	RIR						
	WT						
	REPS		REST	REST	REST	REST	REST
	RIR						

WORKOUT TRACKER

EXERCISE/ MUSCLES

BACK CHEST BICEPS TRICEPS FRONT DELTS REAR DELTS SIDE DELTS QUADS HAMSTRINGS GLUTES CALVES TRAPS ABS

DATE

START TIME

END TIME

	CAD	S1		S2		S3		S4		S5		S6
WT REPS RIR			REST		REST		REST		REST		REST	
WT REPS RIR			REST		REST		REST		REST		REST	
WT REPS RIR			REST		REST		REST		REST		REST	
WT REPS RIR			REST		REST		REST		REST		REST	
WT REPS RIR			REST		REST		REST		REST		REST	
WT REPS RIR			REST		REST		REST		REST		REST	
WT REPS RIR			REST		REST		REST		REST		REST	
WT REPS RIR			REST		REST		REST		REST		REST	
WT REPS RIR			REST		REST		REST		REST		REST	

CAD = Cadence **REPS** = Repetitions

S = Set **RIR** = Repetitions In Reserve

WT = Weight

© ULTIMATE **TRAINING** PLANNER.

WORKOUT TRACKER

DATE

START TIME

END TIME

CAD = Cadence   **REPS** = Repetitions

S = Set   **RIR** = Repetitions in

WT = Weight   Reserve

EXERCISE/ MUSCLES	BACK CHEST BICEPS TRICEPS FRONT DELTS REAR DELTS SIDE DELTS QUADS HAMSTRINGS GLUTES CALVES TRAPS ABS	CAD		S1	S2	S3	S4	S5	S6
		WT							
		REPS							
		RIR							
		WT							
		REPS							
		RIR							
		WT							
		REPS							
		RIR							
		WT							
		REPS							
		RIR							
		WT							
		REPS							
		RIR							
		WT							
		REPS							
		RIR							
		WT							
		REPS							
		RIR							
		WT							
		REPS							
		RIR							

WORKOUT TRACKER

EXERCISE/ MUSCLES

BACK CHEST BICEPS TRICEPS FRONT DELTS REAR DELTS SIDE DELTS QUADS HAMSTRINGS GLUTES CALVES TRAPS ABS

DATE

START TIME

END TIME

	CAD	S1	S2	S3	S4	S5	S6
WT / REPS / RIR			REST	REST	REST	REST	REST
WT / REPS / RIR			REST	REST	REST	REST	REST
WT / REPS / RIR			REST	REST	REST	REST	REST
WT / REPS / RIR			REST	REST	REST	REST	REST
WT / REPS / RIR			REST	REST	REST	REST	REST
WT / REPS / RIR			REST	REST	REST	REST	REST
WT / REPS / RIR			REST	REST	REST	REST	REST
WT / REPS / RIR			REST	REST	REST	REST	REST
WT / REPS / RIR			REST	REST	REST	REST	REST
WT / REPS / RIR			REST	REST	REST	REST	REST

CAD = Cadence
S = Set
WT = Weight
REPS = Repetitions
RIR = Repetitions in reserve

WORKOUT TRACKER

DATE

START TIME

END TIME

CAD = Cadence

S = Set

WT = Weight

REPS = Repetitions

RIR = Repetitions in reserve

EXERCISE/MUSCLES		CAD	S1	S2	S3	S4	S5	S6
BACK CHEST BICEPS TRICEPS FRONT DELTS REAR DELTS SIDE DELTS QUADS HAMSTRINGS GLUTES CALVES TRAPS ABS	WT							
	REPS			REST	REST	REST	REST	REST
	RIR							
	WT							
	REPS			REST	REST	REST	REST	REST
	RIR							
	WT							
	REPS			REST	REST	REST	REST	REST
	RIR							
	WT							
	REPS			REST	REST	REST	REST	REST
	RIR							
	WT							
	REPS			REST	REST	REST	REST	REST
	RIR							
	WT							
	REPS			REST	REST	REST	REST	REST
	RIR							
	WT							
	REPS			REST	REST	REST	REST	REST
	RIR							

WORKOUT TRACKER

EXERCISE/MUSCLES

BACK CHEST BICEPS TRICEPS FRONT DELTS REAR DELTS SIDE DELTS QUADS HAMSTRINGS GLUTES CALVES TRAPS ABS

DATE

START TIME

END TIME

CAD	S1	S2	S3	S4	S5	S6
WT / REPS / RIR		REST	REST	REST	REST	REST

CAD = Cadence

S = Set

WT = Weight

REPS = Repetitions

RIR = Repetitions in reserve

WORKOUT TRACKER

DATE

START TIME

END TIME

CAD = Cadence   **REPS** = Repetitions

S = Set   **RIR** = Repetitions in reserve

WT = Weight

EXERCISE/ MUSCLES

BACK CHEST BICEPS TRICEPS FRONT DELTS REAR DELTS SIDE DELTS QUADS HAMSTRINGS GLUTES CALVES TRAPS ABS

	CAD	S1	S2	S3	S4	S5	S6
WT REPS RIR			REST	REST	REST	REST	REST
WT REPS RIR			REST	REST	REST	REST	REST
WT REPS RIR			REST	REST	REST	REST	REST
WT REPS RIR			REST	REST	REST	REST	REST
WT REPS RIR			REST	REST	REST	REST	REST
WT REPS RIR			REST	REST	REST	REST	REST
WT REPS RIR			REST	REST	REST	REST	REST
WT REPS RIR			REST	REST	REST	REST	REST
WT REPS RIR			REST	REST	REST	REST	REST
WT REPS RIR			REST	REST	REST	REST	REST

WORKOUT TRACKER

DATE

START TIME

END TIME

CAD = Cadence   **REPS** = Repetitions

S = Set   **RIR** = Repetitions in reserve

WT = Weight

EXERCISE/ MUSCLES	CAD		S1	S2	S3	S4	S5	S6
		WT						
		REPS						
		RIR	REST	REST	REST	REST	REST	REST
		WT						
		REPS						
		RIR	REST	REST	REST	REST	REST	REST
		WT						
		REPS						
		RIR	REST	REST	REST	REST	REST	REST
		WT						
		REPS						
		RIR	REST	REST	REST	REST	REST	REST
		WT						
		REPS						
		RIR	REST	REST	REST	REST	REST	REST
		WT						
		REPS						
		RIR	REST	REST	REST	REST	REST	REST
		WT						
		REPS						
		RIR	REST	REST	REST	REST	REST	REST
		WT						
		REPS						
		RIR						

BACK CHEST BICEPS TRICEPS FRONT DELTS REAR DELTS SIDE DELTS QUADS HAMSTRINGS GLUTES CALVES TRAPS ABS

WORKOUT TRACKER

EXERCISE/MUSCLES

BACK CHEST BICEPS TRICEPS FRONT DELTS REAR DELTS SIDE DELTS QUADS HAMSTRINGS GLUTES CALVES TRAPS ABS

DATE

START TIME

END TIME

	CAD	S1	S2	S3	S4	S5	S6
WT / REPS / RIR							
WT / REPS / RIR							
WT / REPS / RIR							
WT / REPS / RIR							
WT / REPS / RIR							
WT / REPS / RIR							
WT / REPS / RIR							
WT / REPS / RIR							
WT / REPS / RIR							
WT / REPS / RIR							

CAD = Cadence **REPS** = Repetitions

S = Set **RIR** = Repetitions in Reserve

WT = Weight

WORKOUT TRACKER

DATE ______ START TIME ______ END TIME ______

CAD = Cadence **REPS** = Repetitions
S = Set **RIR** = Repetitions in reserve
WT = Weight

BACK CHEST BICEPS TRICEPS FRONT DELTS REAR DELTS SIDE DELTS QUADS HAMSTRINGS GLUTES CALVES TRAPS ABS

EXERCISE/ MUSCLES	**CAD**		S1		S2		S3		S4		S5		S6
		WT											
		REPS		REST		REST		REST		REST		REST	
		RIR											
		WT											
		REPS											
		RIR											
		WT											
		REPS		REST		REST		REST		REST		REST	
		RIR											
		WT											
		REPS											
		RIR											
		WT											
		REPS		REST		REST		REST		REST		REST	
		RIR											
		WT											
		REPS											
		RIR											
		WT											
		REPS		REST		REST		REST		REST		REST	
		RIR											
		WT											
		REPS											
		RIR											
		WT											
		REPS		REST		REST		REST		REST		REST	
		RIR											
		WT											
		REPS											
		RIR											

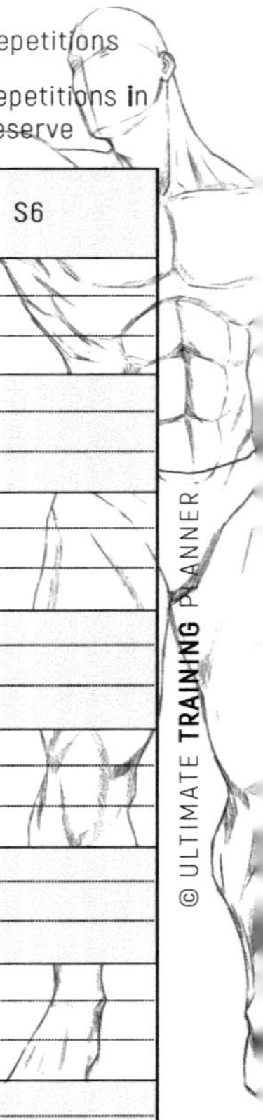

WORKOUT TRACKER

DATE

START TIME

END TIME

CAD = Cadence   **REPS** = Repetitions

S = Set   **RIR** = Repetitions in

WT = Weight   reserve

EXERCISE/
MUSCLES

BACK CHEST BICEPS TRICEPS FRONT DELTS REAR DELTS SIDE DELTS QUADS HAMSTRINGS GLUTES CALVES TRAPS ABS

CAD		S1	S2	S3	S4	S5	S6
WT	REPS						
RIR	REPS	REST	REST	REST	REST	REST	REST

WORKOUT TRACKER

DATE

START TIME

END TIME

CAD = Cadence

S = Set

WT = Weight

REPS = Repetitions

RIR = Repetitions in reserve

BACK CHEST BICEPS TRICEPS FRONT DELTS REAR DELTS SIDE DELTS QUADS HAMSTRINGS GLUTES CALVES TRAPS ABS

EXERCISE/MUSCLES	CAD	S1	S2	S3	S4	S5	S6
	WT						
	REPS		REST	REST	REST	REST	REST
	RIR						
	WT						
	REPS		REST	REST	REST	REST	REST
	RIR						
	WT						
	REPS		REST	REST	REST	REST	REST
	RIR						
	WT						
	REPS		REST	REST	REST	REST	REST
	RIR						
	WT						
	REPS		REST	REST	REST	REST	REST
	RIR						
	WT						
	REPS		REST	REST	REST	REST	REST
	RIR						
	WT						
	REPS		REST	REST	REST	REST	REST
	RIR						
	WT						
	REPS		REST	REST	REST	REST	REST
	RIR						

WORKOUT TRACKER

EXERCISE/ MUSCLES	CAD		S1	S2	S3	S4	S5	S6
		WT						
		REPS						
		RIR						
		WT						
		REPS						
		RIR						
		WT						
		REPS						
		RIR						
		WT						
		REPS						
		RIR						
		WT						
		REPS						
		RIR						
		WT						
		REPS						
		RIR						
		WT						
		REPS						
		RIR						

BACK CHEST BICEPS TRICEPS FRONT DELTS REAR DELTS SIDE DELTS QUADS HAMSTRINGS GLUTES CALVES TRAPS ABS

CAD = Cadence

S = Set

WT = Weight

REPS = Repetitions

RIR = Repetitions in reserve

WORKOUT TRACKER

EXERCISE/MUSCLES	CAD	S1	S2	S3	S4	S5	S6
	WT						
	REPS						
	RIR	REST	REST	REST	REST	REST	REST
	WT						
	REPS						
	RIR	REST	REST	REST	REST	REST	REST
	WT						
	REPS						
	RIR	REST	REST	REST	REST	REST	REST
	WT						
	REPS						
	RIR	REST	REST	REST	REST	REST	REST
	WT						
	REPS						
	RIR	REST	REST	REST	REST	REST	REST
	WT						
	REPS						
	RIR	REST	REST	REST	REST	REST	REST
	WT						
	REPS						
	RIR	REST	REST	REST	REST	REST	REST

BACK CHEST BICEPS TRICEPS FRONT DELTS REAR DELTS SIDE DELTS QUADS HAMSTRINGS GLUTES CALVES TRAPS ABS

DATE

START TIME

END TIME

CAD = Cadence
S = Set
WT = Weight
REPS = Repetitions
RIR = Repetitions In Reserve

WORKOUT TRACKER

EXERCISE/
MUSCLES

BACK CHEST BICEPS TRICEPS FRONT DELTS REAR DELTS SIDE DELTS QUADS HAMSTRINGS GLUTES CALVES TRAPS ABS

DATE

START TIME

END TIME

CAD = Cadence **REPS** = Repetitions
S = Set **RIR** = Repetitions in
WT = Weight Reserve

CAD	S1	S2	S3	S4	S5	S6

WT REPS RIR
WT REPS RIR
WT REPS RIR
WT REPS RIR
WT REPS RIR
WT REPS RIR
WT REPS RIR
WT REPS RIR
WT REPS RIR
WT REPS RIR
WT REPS RIR
WT REPS RIR
WT REPS RIR

REST

WORKOUT TRACKER

EXERCISE/MUSCLES		CAD		S1	S2	S3	S4	S5	S6
	WT								
	REPS					REST	REST	REST	REST
	RIR								
	WT								
	REPS					REST	REST	REST	REST
	RIR								
	WT								
	REPS					REST	REST	REST	REST
	RIR								
	WT								
	REPS					REST	REST	REST	REST
	RIR								
	WT								
	REPS					REST	REST	REST	REST
	RIR								
	WT								
	REPS					REST	REST	REST	REST
	RIR								
	WT								
	REPS					REST	REST	REST	REST
	RIR								
	WT								
	REPS					REST	REST	REST	REST
	RIR								

DATE

START TIME

END TIME

BACK CHEST BICEPS TRICEPS FRONT DELTS REAR DELTS SIDE DELTS QUADS HAMSTRINGS GLUTES CALVES TRAPS ABS

CAD = Cadence   **REPS** = Repetitions
S = Set   **RIR** = Repetitions In Reserve
WT = Weight

WORKOUT TRACKER

EXERCISE/ MUSCLES

BACK CHEST BICEPS TRICEPS FRONT DELTS REAR DELTS SIDE DELTS QUADS HAMSTRINGS GLUTES CALVES TRAPS ABS

DATE

START TIME
END TIME

CAD = Cadence
S = Set
WT = Weight

REPS = Repetitions
RIR = Repetitions in reserve

CAD		S1	S2	S3	S4	S5	S6
	WT						
	REPS						
	RIR						

WORKOUT TRACKER

EXERCISE/
MUSCLES

BACK CHEST BICEPS TRICEPS FRONT DELTS REAR DELTS SIDE DELTS QUADS HAMSTRINGS GLUTES CALVES TRAPS ABS

DATE

START TIME

END TIME

CAD — S1 — S2 — S3 — S4 — S5 — S6

WT — REPS — RIR

REST

CAD = Cadence
S = Set
WT = Weight
REPS = Repetitions
RIR = Repetitions in Reserve

WORKOUT TRACKER

DATE

START TIME

END TIME

EXERCISE/MUSCLES

BACK CHEST BICEPS TRICEPS FRONT DELTS REAR DELTS SIDE DELTS QUADS HAMSTRINGS GLUTES CALVES TRAPS ABS

CAD	S1	S2	S3	S4	S5	S6
WT / REPS / RIR		REST	REST	REST	REST	REST

CAD = Cadence
REPS = Repetitions
S = Set
RIR = Repetitions in Reserve
WT = Weight

WORKOUT TRACKER

EXERCISE/ MUSCLES

DATE

CAD

START TIME

END TIME

	S1	S2	S3	S4	S5	S6
WT / REPS / RIR		REST	REST	REST	REST	REST

CAD = Cadence   REPS = Repetitions

S = Set   RIR = Repetitions in reserve

WT = Weight

© ULTIMATE **TRAINING** PLANNER

WORKOUT TRACKER

DATE

START TIME

END TIME

CAD = Cadence
S = Set
WT = Weight

REPS = Repetitions
RIR = Repetitions In Reserve

EXERCISE/ MUSCLES

BACK CHEST BICEPS TRICEPS FRONT DELTS REAR DELTS SIDE DELTS QUADS HAMSTRINGS GLUTES CALVES TRAPS ABS

CAD	S1	S2	S3	S4	S5	S6
WT						
REPS						
RIR						

WORKOUT TRACKER

DATE

START TIME

END TIME

CAD = Cadence
S = Set
WT = Weight
REPS = Repetitions
RIR = Repetitions in reserve

EXERCISE/ MUSCLES	CAD	S1	S2	S3	S4	S5	S6
	WT		REST	REST	REST	REST	REST
	REPS						
	RIR						
	WT		REST	REST	REST	REST	REST
	REPS						
	RIR						
	WT		REST	REST	REST	REST	REST
	REPS						
	RIR						
	WT		REST	REST	REST	REST	REST
	REPS						
	RIR						
	WT		REST	REST	REST	REST	REST
	REPS						
	RIR						
	WT		REST	REST	REST	REST	REST
	REPS						
	RIR						
	WT		REST	REST	REST	REST	REST
	REPS						
	RIR						
	WT		REST	REST	REST	REST	REST
	REPS						
	RIR						
	WT		REST	REST	REST	REST	REST
	REPS						
	RIR						

BACK CHEST BICEPS TRICEPS FRONT DELTS REAR DELTS SIDE DELTS QUADS HAMSTRINGS GLUTES CALVES TRAPS ABS

WORKOUT TRACKER

EXERCISE/ MUSCLES

BACK CHEST BICEPS TRICEPS FRONT DELTS REAR DELTS SIDE DELTS QUADS HAMSTRINGS GLUTES CALVES TRAPS ABS

DATE

START TIME

END TIME

CAD = Cadence

S = Set

WT = Weight

REPS = Repetitions

RIR = Repetitions In Reserve

CAD	S1	S2	S3	S4	S5	S6
WT						
REPS						
RIR	REST	REST	REST	REST	REST	REST
WT						
REPS						
RIR	REST	REST	REST	REST	REST	REST
WT						
REPS						
RIR	REST	REST	REST	REST	REST	REST
WT						
REPS						
RIR	REST	REST	REST	REST	REST	REST
WT						
REPS						
RIR	REST	REST	REST	REST	REST	REST
WT						
REPS						
RIR	REST	REST	REST	REST	REST	REST
WT						
REPS						
RIR	REST	REST	REST	REST	REST	REST
WT						
REPS						
RIR	REST	REST	REST	REST	REST	REST

WORKOUT TRACKER

DATE

START TIME

END TIME

CAD = Cadence

S = Set

WT = Weight

REPS = Repetitions

RIR = Repetitions in Reserve

EXERCISE/ MUSCLES	CAD		S1	S2	S3	S4	S5	S6
		WT						
		REPS						
		RIR						
		WT						
		REPS						
		RIR						
		WT						
		REPS						
		RIR						
		WT						
		REPS						
		RIR						
		WT						
		REPS						
		RIR						
		WT						
		REPS						
		RIR						
		WT						
		REPS						
		RIR						
		WT						
		REPS						
		RIR						
		WT						
		REPS						
		RIR						
		WT						
		REPS						
		RIR						

REST REST REST REST REST

BACK CHEST BICEPS TRICEPS FRONT DELTS REAR DELTS SIDE DELTS QUADS HAMSTRINGS GLUTES CALVES TRAPS ABS

WORKOUT TRACKER

DATE

START TIME

END TIME

CAD	REPS = Repetitions
CAD = Cadence	**REPS** = Repetitions
S = Set	**RIR** = Repetitions in reserve
WT = Weight	

EXERCISE/ MUSCLES

BACK CHEST BICEPS TRICEPS FRONT DELTS REAR DELTS SIDE DELTS QUADS HAMSTRINGS GLUTES CALVES TRAPS ABS

	CAD	S1	S2	S3	S4	S5	S6
	WT						
	REPS						
	RIR						

WORKOUT TRACKER

EXERCISE/ MUSCLES

BACK CHEST BICEPS TRICEPS FRONT DELTS REAR DELTS SIDE DELTS QUADS HAMSTRINGS GLUTES CALVES TRAPS ABS

DATE

START TIME

END TIME

CAD	S1	S2	S3	S4	S5	S6

WT / REPS / RIR

REST

CAD = Cadence **REPS** = Repetitions
S = Set **RIR** = Repetitions in
WT = Weight reserve

© ULTIMATE **TRAINING** PLANNER

WORKOUT TRACKER

DATE

START TIME

END TIME

CAD = Cadence   **REPS** = Repetitions

S = Set   **RIR** = Repetitions in reserve

WT = Weight

EXERCISE/ MUSCLES

BACK   CHEST   BICEPS   TRICEPS   FRONT DELTS   REAR DELTS   SIDE DELTS   QUADS   HAMSTRINGS   GLUTES   CALVES   TRAPS   ABS

CAD	S1	S2	S3	S4	S5	S6
WT REPS RIR						
WT REPS RIR						
WT REPS RIR						
WT REPS RIR						
WT REPS RIR						
WT REPS RIR						
WT REPS RIR						
WT REPS RIR						
WT REPS RIR						
WT REPS RIR						
WT REPS RIR						
WT REPS RIR						

WORKOUT TRACKER

DATE | START TIME | END TIME

CAD = Cadence **REPS** = Repetitions
S = Set **RIR** = Repetitions in reserve
WT = Weight

BACK CHEST BICEPS TRICEPS FRONT DELTS REAR DELTS SIDE DELTS QUADS HAMSTRINGS GLUTES CALVES TRAPS ABS

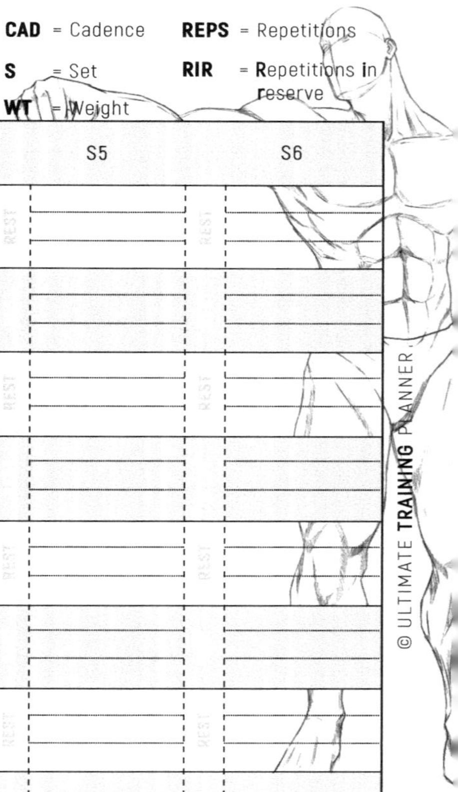

EXERCISE/ MUSCLES	CAD		S1		S2		S3		S4		S5		S6
		WT											
		REPS		REST		REST		REST		REST		REST	
		RIR											
		WT											
		REPS											
		RIR											
		WT											
		REPS		REST		REST		REST		REST		REST	
		RIR											
		WT											
		REPS											
		RIR											
		WT											
		REPS		REST		REST		REST		REST		REST	
		RIR											
		WT											
		REPS											
		RIR											
		WT											
		REPS		REST		REST		REST		REST		REST	
		RIR											
		WT											
		REPS											
		RIR											
		WT											
		REPS		REST		REST		REST		REST		REST	
		RIR											
		WT											
		REPS											
		RIR											

© ULTIMATE TRAINING PLANNER.

WORKOUT TRACKER

EXERCISE/ MUSCLES		CAD		S1	S2	S3	S4	S5	S6
			WT						
			REPS		REST	REST	REST	REST	REST
			RIR						
			WT						
			REPS		REST	REST	REST	REST	REST
			RIR						
			WT						
			REPS		REST	REST	REST	REST	REST
			RIR						
			WT						
			REPS		REST	REST	REST	REST	REST
			RIR						
			WT						
			REPS		REST	REST	REST	REST	REST
			RIR						
			WT						
			REPS		REST	REST	REST	REST	REST
			RIR						
			WT						
			REPS		REST	REST	REST	REST	REST
			RIR						

DATE

BACK CHEST BICEPS TRICEPS FRONT DELTS REAR DELTS SIDE DELTS QUADS HAMSTRINGS GLUTES CALVES TRAPS ABS

START TIME

END TIME

CAD = Cadence

S = Set

WT = Weight

REPS = Repetitions

RIR = Repetitions In Reserve

WORKOUT TRACKER

DATE

START TIME

END TIME

EXERCISE/ MUSCLES	CAD		S1		S2		S3		S4		S5		S6
		REPS											
		WT											
		RIR		REST		REST		REST		REST		REST	
		REPS											
		WT											
		RIR		REST		REST		REST		REST		REST	
		REPS											
		WT											
		RIR		REST		REST		REST		REST		REST	
		REPS											
		WT											
		RIR		REST		REST		REST		REST		REST	
		REPS											
		WT											
		RIR		REST		REST		REST		REST		REST	
		REPS											
		WT											
		RIR		REST		REST		REST		REST		REST	
		REPS											
		WT											
		RIR											

BACK CHEST BICEPS TRICEPS FRONT DELTS REAR DELTS SIDE DELTS QUADS HAMSTRINGS GLUTES CALVES TRAPS ABS

CAD = Cadence

S = Set

WT = Weight

REPS = Repetitions

RIR = Repetitions in reserve

WORKOUT TRACKER

EXERCISE/MUSCLES

BACK · CHEST · BICEPS · TRICEPS · FRONT DELTS · REAR DELTS · SIDE DELTS · QUADS · HAMSTRINGS · GLUTES · CALVES · TRAPS · ABS

DATE

START TIME   END TIME

CAD = Cadence   **REPS** = Repetitions
S = Set   **RIR** = Repetitions in reserve
WT = Weight

	CAD	S1	S2	S3	S4	S5	S6
WT							
REPS							
RIR		REST	REST	REST	REST	REST	REST

WORKOUT TRACKER

© ULTIMATE **TRAINING** PLANNER

EXERCISE/ MUSCLES	CAD		S1	S2	S3	S4	S5	S6
		WT						
		REPS						
		RIR						
		WT		REST	REST	REST	REST	REST
		REPS						
		RIR						
		WT						
		REPS						
		RIR		REST	REST	REST	REST	REST
		WT						
		REPS						
		RIR						
		WT		REST	REST	REST	REST	REST
		REPS						
		RIR						
		WT						
		REPS						
		RIR		REST	REST	REST	REST	REST
		WT						
		REPS						
		RIR						

BACK CHEST BICEPS TRICEPS FRONT DELTS REAR DELTS SIDE DELTS QUADS HAMSTRINGS GLUTES CALVES TRAPS ABS

DATE

START TIME

END TIME

CAD = Cadence

S = Set

WT = Weight

REPS = Repetitions

RIR = Repetitions in reserve

WORKOUT TRACKER

EXERCISE/ MUSCLES

BACK CHEST BICEPS TRICEPS FRONT DELTS REAR DELTS SIDE DELTS QUADS HAMSTRINGS GLUTES CALVES TRAPS ABS

DATE

START TIME   END TIME

CAD	S1	S2	S3	S4	S5	S6

WT / REPS / RIR

REST

CAD = Cadence   **REPS** = Repetitions

S = Set   **RIR** = Repetitions in reserve

WT = Weight

WORKOUT TRACKER

EXERCISE/MUSCLES

BACK CHEST BICEPS TRICEPS FRONT DELTS REAR DELTS SIDE DELTS QUADS HAMSTRINGS GLUTES CALVES TRAPS ABS

DATE

START TIME

END TIME

CAD	S1	S2	S3	S4	S5	S6
WT / REPS / RIR	REST	REST	REST	REST	REST	REST

CAD = Cadence
S = Set
WT = Weight
REPS = Repetitions
RIR = Repetitions in Reserve

WORKOUT TRACKER

DATE

START TIME

END TIME

CAD = Cadence

REPS = Repetitions

S = Set

RIR = Repetitions in Reserve

WT = Weight

EXERCISE/ MUSCLES

BACK CHEST BICEPS TRICEPS FRONT DELTS REAR DELTS SIDE DELTS QUADS HAMSTRINGS GLUTES CALVES TRAPS ABS

CAD	S1	S2	S3	S4	S5	S6
WT / REPS / RIR	REST	REST	REST	REST	REST	

WORKOUT TRACKER

EXERCISE/MUSCLES

BACK CHEST BICEPS TRICEPS FRONT DELTS REAR DELTS SIDE DELTS QUADS HAMSTRINGS GLUTES CALVES TRAPS ABS

DATE

START TIME

END TIME

	CAD	S1	S2	S3	S4	S5	S6
WT / REPS / RIR			REST	REST	REST	REST	REST
WT / REPS / RIR			REST	REST	REST	REST	REST
WT / REPS / RIR			REST	REST	REST	REST	REST
WT / REPS / RIR			REST	REST	REST	REST	REST
WT / REPS / RIR			REST	REST	REST	REST	REST
WT / REPS / RIR			REST	REST	REST	REST	REST
WT / REPS / RIR			REST	REST	REST	REST	REST
WT / REPS / RIR			REST	REST	REST	REST	REST
WT / REPS / RIR			REST	REST	REST	REST	REST
WT / REPS / RIR			REST	REST	REST	REST	REST
WT / REPS / RIR			REST	REST	REST	REST	REST
WT / REPS / RIR			REST	REST	REST	REST	REST

CAD = Cadence
S = Set
WT = Weight
REPS = Repetitions
RIR = Repetitions In reserve

© ULTIMATE **TRAINING** PLANNER

WORKOUT TRACKER

EXERCISE/ MUSCLES

BACK CHEST BICEPS TRICEPS FRONT DELTS REAR DELTS SIDE DELTS QUADS HAMSTRINGS GLUTES CALVES TRAPS ABS

DATE

START TIME

END TIME

CAD = Cadence **REPS** = Repetitions

S = Set

WT = Weight

RIR = Repetitions In reserve

CAD		S1	S2	S3	S4	S5	S6
WT							
REPS							
RIR		REST	REST	REST	REST	REST	
WT							
REPS							
RIR		REST	REST	REST	REST	REST	
WT							
REPS							
RIR		REST	REST	REST	REST	REST	
WT							
REPS							
RIR		REST	REST	REST	REST	REST	
WT							
REPS							
RIR		REST	REST	REST	REST	REST	
WT							
REPS							
RIR		REST	REST	REST	REST	REST	
WT							
REPS							
RIR		REST	REST	REST	REST	REST	

WORKOUT TRACKER

EXERCISE/ MUSCLES		CAD		S1		S2		S3		S4		S5		S6
	WT													
	REPS			REST		REST		REST		REST		REST		
	RIR													
	WT													
	REPS			REST		REST		REST		REST		REST		
	RIR													
	WT													
	REPS			REST		REST		REST		REST		REST		
	RIR													
	WT													
	REPS			REST		REST		REST		REST		REST		
	RIR													
	WT													
	REPS			REST		REST		REST		REST		REST		
	RIR													
	WT													
	REPS			REST		REST		REST		REST		REST		
	RIR													
	WT													
	REPS			REST		REST		REST		REST		REST		
	RIR													
	WT													
	REPS			REST		REST		REST		REST		REST		
	RIR													

DATE

START TIME

END TIME

BACK CHEST BICEPS TRICEPS FRONT DELTS REAR DELTS SIDE DELTS QUADS HAMSTRINGS GLUTES CALVES TRAPS ABS

CAD = Cadence

S = Set

WT = Weight

REPS = Repetitions

RIR = Repetitions in reserve

WORKOUT TRACKER

EXERCISE/
MUSCLES

BACK CHEST BICEPS TRICEPS FRONT DELTS REAR DELTS SIDE DELTS QUADS HAMSTRINGS GLUTES CALVES TRAPS ABS

DATE

START TIME

END TIME

	CAD	S1	S2	S3	S4	S5	S6
WT REPS RIR							
WT REPS RIR							
WT REPS RIR							
WT REPS RIR							
WT REPS RIR							
WT REPS RIR							
WT REPS RIR							
WT REPS RIR							
WT REPS RIR							
WT REPS RIR							
WT REPS RIR							

CAD = Cadence   **REPS** = Repetitions

S = Set   **RIR** = Repetitions in Reserve

WT = Weight

WORKOUT TRACKER

EXERCISE/ MUSCLES

BACK · CHEST · BICEPS · TRICEPS · FRONT DELTS · REAR DELTS · SIDE DELTS · QUADS · HAMSTRINGS · GLUTES · CALVES · TRAPS · ABS

DATE

START TIME

END TIME

CAD	S1	S2	S3	S4	S5	S6

REPS · WT · RIR

REST

CAD = Cadence
S = Set
WT = Weight
REPS = Repetitions
RIR = Repetitions in reserve

WORKOUT TRACKER

DATE

START TIME

END TIME

CAD = Cadence

REPS = Repetitions

S = Set

RIR = Repetitions In Reserve

WT = Weight

EXERCISE/ MUSCLES

BACK CHEST BICEPS TRICEPS FRONT DELTS REAR DELTS SIDE DELTS QUADS HAMSTRINGS GLUTES CALVES TRAPS ABS

	CAD	S1	S2	S3	S4	S5	S6
WT REPS RIR			REST	REST	REST	REST	REST
WT REPS RIR			REST	REST	REST	REST	REST
WT REPS RIR			REST	REST	REST	REST	REST
WT REPS RIR			REST	REST	REST	REST	REST
WT REPS RIR			REST	REST	REST	REST	REST
WT REPS RIR			REST	REST	REST	REST	REST
WT REPS RIR			REST	REST	REST	REST	REST
WT REPS RIR			REST	REST	REST	REST	REST
WT REPS RIR			REST	REST	REST	REST	REST

WORKOUT TRACKER

DATE ____________ START TIME ______ END TIME ______

CAD = Cadence **REPS** = Repetitions
S = Set **RIR** = Repetitions in reserve
WT = Weight

BACK CHEST BICEPS TRICEPS FRONT DELTS REAR DELTS SIDE DELTS QUADS HAMSTRINGS GLUTES CALVES TRAPS ABS

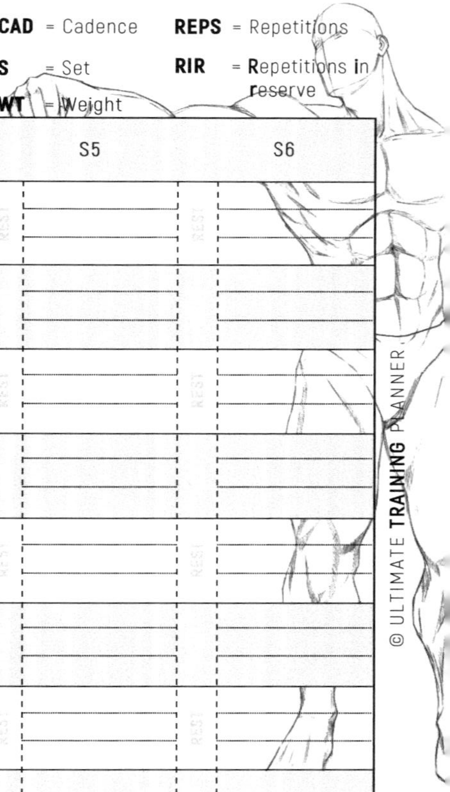

EXERCISE/ MUSCLES	CAD		S1		S2		S3		S4		S5		S6
		WT											
		REPS		REST		REST		REST		REST		REST	
		RIR											
		WT											
		REPS											
		RIR											
		WT											
		REPS		REST		REST		REST		REST		REST	
		RIR											
		WT											
		REPS											
		RIR											
		WT											
		REPS		REST		REST		REST		REST		REST	
		RIR											
		WT											
		REPS											
		RIR											
		WT											
		REPS		REST		REST		REST		REST		REST	
		RIR											
		WT											
		REPS											
		RIR											
		WT											
		REPS		REST		REST		REST		REST		REST	
		RIR											
		WT											
		REPS											
		RIR											

WORKOUT TRACKER

DATE

START TIME

END TIME

CAD = Cadence

S = Set

WT = Weight

REPS = Repetitions

RIR = Repetitions In Reserve

EXERCISE/ MUSCLES

BACK CHEST BICEPS TRICEPS FRONT DELTS REAR DELTS SIDE DELTS QUADS HAMSTRINGS GLUTES CALVES TRAPS ABS

	CAD	S1	S2	S3	S4	S5	S6
WT / REPS / RIR			REST	REST	REST	REST	REST
WT / REPS / RIR			REST	REST	REST	REST	REST
WT / REPS / RIR			REST	REST	REST	REST	REST
WT / REPS / RIR			REST	REST	REST	REST	REST
WT / REPS / RIR			REST	REST	REST	REST	REST
WT / REPS / RIR			REST	REST	REST	REST	REST
WT / REPS / RIR			REST	REST	REST	REST	REST
WT / REPS / RIR			REST	REST	REST	REST	REST
WT / REPS / RIR			REST	REST	REST	REST	REST
WT / REPS / RIR			REST	REST	REST	REST	REST
WT / REPS / RIR			REST	REST	REST	REST	REST
WT / REPS / RIR			REST	REST	REST	REST	REST

WORKOUT TRACKER

EXERCISE/ MUSCLES

BACK CHEST BICEPS TRICEPS FRONT DELTS REAR DELTS SIDE DELTS QUADS HAMSTRINGS GLUTES CALVES TRAPS ABS

DATE

START TIME

END TIME

CAD = Cadence
S = Set
WT = Weight
REPS = Repetitions
RIR = Repetitions In reserve

CAD		S1	S2	S3	S4	S5	S6
WT			REST	REST	REST	REST	REST
REPS							
RIR							
WT			REST	REST	REST	REST	REST
REPS							
RIR							
WT			REST	REST	REST	REST	REST
REPS							
RIR							
WT			REST	REST	REST	REST	REST
REPS							
RIR							
WT			REST	REST	REST	REST	REST
REPS							
RIR							
WT			REST	REST	REST	REST	REST
REPS							
RIR							
WT			REST	REST	REST	REST	REST
REPS							
RIR							

WORKOUT TRACKER

EXERCISE/MUSCLES

BACK · CHEST · BICEPS · TRICEPS · FRONT DELTS · REAR DELTS · SIDE DELTS · QUADS · HAMSTRINGS · GLUTES · CALVES · TRAPS · ABS

DATE

START TIME

END TIME

	CAD	S1	S2	S3	S4	S5	S6
WT / REPS / RIR			REST	REST	REST	REST	REST
WT / REPS / RIR							
WT / REPS / RIR							
WT / REPS / RIR							
WT / REPS / RIR							
WT / REPS / RIR							
WT / REPS / RIR							
WT / REPS / RIR							

CAD = Cadence   REPS = Repetitions

S = Set   RIR = Repetitions in Reserve

WT = Weight

WORKOUT TRACKER

EXERCISE/ MUSCLES

BACK CHEST BICEPS TRICEPS FRONT DELTS REAR DELTS SIDE DELTS QUADS HAMSTRINGS GLUTES CALVES TRAPS ABS

DATE

START TIME

END TIME

CAD = Cadence

S = Set

WT = Weight

REPS = Repetitions

RIR = Repetitions in reserve

CAD	S1	S2	S3	S4	S5	S6
WT						
REPS						
RIR	REST	REST	REST	REST	REST	REST
WT						
REPS						
RIR	REST	REST	REST	REST	REST	REST
WT						
REPS						
RIR	REST	REST	REST	REST	REST	REST
WT						
REPS						
RIR	REST	REST	REST	REST	REST	REST
WT						
REPS						
RIR	REST	REST	REST	REST	REST	REST
WT						
REPS						
RIR	REST	REST	REST	REST	REST	REST
WT						
REPS						
RIR	REST	REST	REST	REST	REST	REST

WORKOUT TRACKER

EXERCISE/ MUSCLES

BACK CHEST BICEPS TRICEPS FRONT DELTS REAR DELTS SIDE DELTS QUADS HAMSTRINGS GLUTES CALVES TRAPS ABS

DATE

START TIME

END TIME

CAD	S1	S2	S3	S4	S5	S6
WT						
REPS						
RIR						

CAD = Cadence
S = Set
WT = Weight
REPS = Repetitions
RIR = Repetitions In Reserve

REST

WORKOUT TRACKER

DATE

START TIME

END TIME

CAD = Cadence

S = Set

WT = Weight

REPS = Repetitions

RIR = Repetitions in Reserve

EXERCISE/ MUSCLES

BACK CHEST BICEPS TRICEPS FRONT DELTS REAR DELTS SIDE DELTS QUADS HAMSTRINGS GLUTES CALVES TRAPS ABS

CAD	S1	S2	S3	S4	S5	S6
WT REPS RIR						

REST

WORKOUT TRACKER

EXERCISE/ MUSCLES

BACK CHEST BICEPS TRICEPS FRONT DELTS REAR DELTS SIDE DELTS QUADS HAMSTRINGS GLUTES CALVES TRAPS ABS

DATE

START TIME END TIME

CAD	S1	S2	S3	S4	S5	S6
WT / REPS / RIR		REST	REST	REST	REST	REST

CAD = Cadence **REPS** = Repetitions
S = Set **RIR** = Repetitions in reserve
WT = Weight

© ULTIMATE **TRAINING** PLANNER

WORKOUT TRACKER

EXERCISE/MUSCLES		CAD	S1	S2	S3	S4	S5	S6
	WT							
	REPS			REST	REST	REST	REST	REST
	RIR							
	WT							
	REPS		REST	REST	REST	REST	REST	REST
	RIR							
	WT							
	REPS		REST	REST	REST	REST	REST	REST
	RIR							
	WT							
	REPS		REST	REST	REST	REST	REST	REST
	RIR							
	WT							
	REPS		REST	REST	REST	REST	REST	REST
	RIR							
	WT							
	REPS		REST	REST	REST	REST	REST	REST
	RIR							
	WT							
	REPS		REST	REST	REST	REST	REST	REST
	RIR							

BACK CHEST BICEPS TRICEPS FRONT DELTS REAR DELTS SIDE DELTS QUADS HAMSTRINGS GLUTES CALVES TRAPS ABS

DATE

START TIME

END TIME

CAD = Cadence
S = Set
WT = Weight
REPS = Repetitions
RIR = Repetitions In reserve

WORKOUT TRACKER

DATE | START TIME | END TIME

CAD = Cadence **REPS** = Repetitions
S = Set **RIR** = Repetitions in reserve
WT = Weight

BACK CHEST BICEPS TRICEPS FRONT DELTS REAR DELTS SIDE DELTS QUADS HAMSTRINGS GLUTES CALVES TRAPS ABS

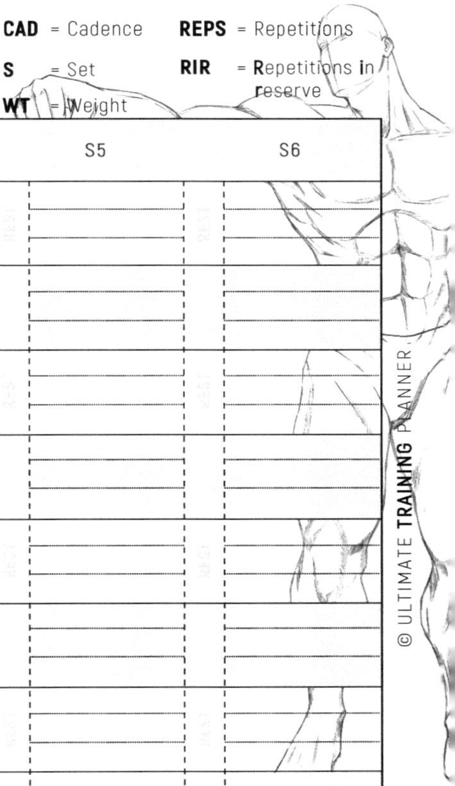

EXERCISE/ MUSCLES	CAD		S1		S2		S3		S4		S5		S6
		WT											
		REPS		REST		REST		REST		REST		REST	
		RIR											
		WT											
		REPS											
		RIR											
		WT											
		REPS		REST		REST		REST		REST		REST	
		RIR											
		WT											
		REPS											
		RIR											
		WT											
		REPS		REST		REST		REST		REST		REST	
		RIR											
		WT											
		REPS											
		RIR											
		WT											
		REPS		REST		REST		REST		REST		REST	
		RIR											
		WT											
		REPS											
		RIR											
		WT											
		REPS		REST		REST		REST		REST		REST	
		RIR											
		WT											
		REPS											
		RIR											

WORKOUT TRACKER

© ULTIMATE **TRAINING** PLANNER

DATE [   ]

START TIME [   ]

END TIME [   ]

EXERCISE/ MUSCLES

BACK CHEST BICEPS TRICEPS FRONT DELTS REAR DELTS SIDE DELTS QUADS HAMSTRINGS GLUTES CALVES TRAPS ABS

CAD = Cadence **REPS** = Repetitions
S = Set **RIR** = Repetitions in reserve
WT = Weight

EXERCISE/MUSCLES	CAD	S1			S2			S3			S4			S5			S6		
		WT	REPS	RIR	WT	REPS	RIR	WT	REPS	RIR	WT	REPS	RIR	WT	REPS	RIR	WT	REPS	RIR
					REST			REST			REST			REST			REST		
					REST			REST			REST			REST			REST		
					REST			REST			REST			REST			REST		
					REST			REST			REST			REST			REST		
					REST			REST			REST			REST			REST		
					REST			REST			REST			REST			REST		
					REST			REST			REST			REST			REST		

WORKOUT TRACKER

DATE

START TIME

END TIME

CAD = Cadence
S = Set
WT = Weight
REPS = Repetitions
RIR = Repetitions in reserve

BACK CHEST BICEPS TRICEPS FRONT DELTS REAR DELTS SIDE DELTS QUADS HAMSTRINGS GLUTES CALVES TRAPS ABS

EXERCISE/ MUSCLES	**CAD**		S1		S2		S3		S4		S5		S6
		WT											
		REPS		REST		REST		REST		REST		REST	
		RIR											
		WT											
		REPS											
		RIR											
		WT											
		REPS		REST		REST		REST		REST		REST	
		RIR											
		WT											
		REPS											
		RIR											
		WT											
		REPS		REST		REST		REST		REST		REST	
		RIR											
		WT											
		REPS											
		RIR											
		WT											
		REPS		REST		REST		REST		REST		REST	
		RIR											
		WT											
		REPS											
		RIR											
		WT											
		REPS		REST		REST		REST		REST		REST	
		RIR											
		WT											
		REPS											
		RIR											

© ULTIMATE **TRAINING** PLANNER

WORKOUT TRACKER

EXERCISE/ MUSCLES

BACK CHEST BICEPS TRICEPS FRONT DELTS REAR DELTS SIDE DELTS QUADS HAMSTRINGS GLUTES CALVES TRAPS ABS

DATE

START TIME

END TIME

	CAD	S1	S2	S3	S4	S5	S6
WT REPS RIR			REST	REST	REST	REST	REST
WT REPS RIR			REST	REST	REST	REST	REST
WT REPS RIR			REST	REST	REST	REST	REST
WT REPS RIR			REST	REST	REST	REST	REST
WT REPS RIR			REST	REST	REST	REST	REST
WT REPS RIR			REST	REST	REST	REST	REST
WT REPS RIR			REST	REST	REST	REST	REST
WT REPS RIR			REST	REST	REST	REST	REST

CAD = Cadence
S = Set
WT = Weight
REPS = Repetitions
RIR = Repetitions in reserve

WORKOUT TRACKER

DATE

START TIME

END TIME

CAD = Cadence

REPS = Repetitions

S = Set

RIR = Repetitions in reserve

WT = Weight

EXERCISE/ MUSCLES	CAD		S1	S2	S3	S4	S5	S6
		WT						
		REPS						
		RIR	REST	REST	REST	REST	REST	REST
		WT						
		REPS						
		RIR	REST	REST	REST	REST	REST	REST
		WT						
		REPS						
		RIR	REST	REST	REST	REST	REST	REST
		WT						
		REPS						
		RIR	REST	REST	REST	REST	REST	REST
		WT						
		REPS						
		RIR	REST	REST	REST	REST	REST	REST
		WT						
		REPS						
		RIR	REST	REST	REST	REST	REST	REST
		WT						
		REPS						
		RIR	REST	REST	REST	REST	REST	REST
		WT						
		REPS						
		RIR	REST	REST	REST	REST	REST	REST

BACK CHEST BICEPS TRICEPS FRONT DELTS REAR DELTS SIDE DELTS QUADS HAMSTRINGS GLUTES CALVES TRAPS ABS

WORKOUT TRACKER

EXERCISE/ MUSCLES

BACK CHEST BICEPS TRICEPS FRONT DELTS REAR DELTS SIDE DELTS QUADS HAMSTRINGS GLUTES CALVES TRAPS ABS

DATE

START TIME

END TIME

CAD = Cadence
S = Set
WT = Weight
REPS = Repetitions
RIR = Repetitions in reserve

CAD	S1	S2	S3	S4	S5	S6
WT						
REPS						
RIR						

REST

WORKOUT TRACKER

BACK CHEST BICEPS TRICEPS FRONT DELTS REAR DELTS SIDE DELTS QUADS HAMSTRINGS GLUTES CALVES TRAPS ABS

EXERCISE/ MUSCLES

START TIME
END TIME

CAD = Cadence **REPS** = Repetitions
S = Set
WT = Weight **RIR** = Repetitions in reserve

EXERCISE/ MUSCLES	CAD	S1	S2	S3	S4	S5	S6
	WT						
	REPS						
	RIR						
	WT						
	REPS						
	RIR						
	WT						
	REPS						
	RIR						
	WT						
	REPS						
	RIR						
	WT						
	REPS						
	RIR						
	WT						
	REPS						
	RIR						
	WT						
	REPS						
	RIR						
	WT						
	REPS						
	RIR						
	WT						
	REPS						
	RIR						
	WT						
	REPS						
	RIR						

WORKOUT TRACKER

EXERCISE/ MUSCLES

BACK CHEST BICEPS TRICEPS FRONT DELTS REAR DELTS SIDE DELTS QUADS HAMSTRINGS GLUTES CALVES TRAPS ABS

DATE

START TIME

END TIME

CAD	S1	S2	S3	S4	S5	S6
WT / REPS / RIR						

REST

CAD = Cadence
S = Set
WT = Weight
REPS = Repetitions
RIR = Repetitions in reserve

WORKOUT TRACKER

DATE

START TIME

END TIME

CAD = Cadence

S = Set **WT** = Weight

REPS = Repetitions

RIR = Repetitions In Reserve

EXERCISE/ MUSCLES

BACK CHEST BICEPS TRICEPS FRONT DELTS REAR DELTS SIDE DELTS QUADS HAMSTRINGS GLUTES CALVES TRAPS ABS

EXERCISE/MUSCLES	CAD	S1	S2	S3	S4	S5	S6
	WT						
	REPS						
	RIR	REST	REST	REST	REST	REST	
	WT						
	REPS						
	RIR	REST	REST	REST	REST	REST	
	WT						
	REPS						
	RIR	REST	REST	REST	REST	REST	
	WT						
	REPS						
	RIR	REST	REST	REST	REST	REST	
	WT						
	REPS						
	RIR	REST	REST	REST	REST	REST	
	WT						
	REPS						
	RIR	REST	REST	REST	REST	REST	

WORKOUT TRACKER

EXERCISE/ MUSCLES	CAD			S1			S2			S3			S4			S5			S6		
	WT	REPS	RIR																		
	WT	REPS	RIR					REST				REST				REST				REST		
	WT	REPS	RIR																		
	WT	REPS	RIR					REST				REST				REST				REST		
	WT	REPS	RIR																		
	WT	REPS	RIR					REST				REST				REST				REST		
	WT	REPS	RIR																		
	WT	REPS	RIR					REST				REST				REST				REST		
	WT	REPS	RIR																		
	WT	REPS	RIR					REST				REST				REST				REST		

BACK CHEST BICEPS TRICEPS FRONT DELTS REAR DELTS SIDE DELTS QUADS HAMSTRINGS GLUTES CALVES TRAPS ABS

DATE

START TIME

END TIME

CAD = Cadence

S = Set

WT = Weight

REPS = Repetitions

RIR = Repetitions In reserve

© ULTIMATE **TRAINING** PLANNER

WORKOUT TRACKER

EXERCISE/MUSCLES

BACK CHEST BICEPS TRICEPS FRONT DELTS REAR DELTS SIDE DELTS QUADS HAMSTRINGS GLUTES CALVES TRAPS ABS

DATE

START TIME | END TIME

	CAD	S1	S2	S3	S4	S5	S6
WT							
REPS							
RIR			REST	REST	REST	REST	REST
WT							
REPS							
RIR			REST	REST	REST	REST	REST
WT							
REPS							
RIR			REST	REST	REST	REST	REST
WT							
REPS							
RIR			REST	REST	REST	REST	REST
WT							
REPS							
RIR			REST	REST	REST	REST	REST
WT							
REPS							
RIR			REST	REST	REST	REST	REST
WT							
REPS							
RIR			REST	REST	REST	REST	REST
WT							
REPS							
RIR			REST	REST	REST	REST	REST
WT							
REPS							
RIR			REST	REST	REST	REST	REST

CAD = Cadence **REPS** = Repetitions
S = Set **RIR** = Repetitions in reserve
WT = Weight

WORKOUT TRACKER

EXERCISE/MUSCLES		CAD		S1		S2		S3		S4		S5		S6
	WT				REST		REST		REST		REST		REST	
	REPS													
	RIR													
	WT				REST		REST		REST		REST		REST	
	REPS													
	RIR													
	WT				REST		REST		REST		REST		REST	
	REPS													
	RIR													
	WT				REST		REST		REST		REST		REST	
	REPS													
	RIR													
	WT				REST		REST		REST		REST		REST	
	REPS													
	RIR													
	WT				REST		REST		REST		REST		REST	
	REPS													
	RIR													

BACK CHEST BICEPS TRICEPS FRONT DELTS REAR DELTS SIDE DELTS QUADS HAMSTRINGS GLUTES CALVES TRAPS ABS

DATE

START TIME

END TIME

CAD = Cadence

S = Set

WT = Weight

REPS = Repetitions

RIR = Repetitions in reserve

WORKOUT TRACKER

BACK CHEST BICEPS TRICEPS FRONT DELTS REAR DELTS SIDE DELTS QUADS HAMSTRINGS GLUTES CALVES TRAPS ABS

EXERCISE/MUSCLES

DATE

START TIME

END TIME

CAD	S1	S2	S3	S4	S5	S6

WT / REPS / RIR

REST

CAD = Cadence

REPS = Repetitions

S = Set

RIR = Repetitions in Reserve

WT = Weight

WORKOUT TRACKER

DATE

START TIME

END TIME

CAD = Cadence
S = Set
WT = Weight
REPS = Repetitions
RIR = Repetitions in reserve

BACK CHEST BICEPS TRICEPS FRONT DELTS REAR DELTS SIDE DELTS QUADS HAMSTRINGS GLUTES CALVES TRAPS ABS

EXERCISE/ MUSCLES	CAD		S1		S2		S3		S4		S5		S6
		WT											
		REPS		REST		REST		REST		REST		REST	
		RIR											
		WT											
		REPS											
		RIR											
		WT											
		REPS		REST		REST		REST		REST		REST	
		RIR											
		WT											
		REPS											
		RIR											
		WT											
		REPS		REST		REST		REST		REST		REST	
		RIR											
		WT											
		REPS											
		RIR											
		WT											
		REPS		REST		REST		REST		REST		REST	
		RIR											
		WT											
		REPS											
		RIR											
		WT											
		REPS		REST		REST		REST		REST		REST	
		RIR											
		WT											
		REPS											
		RIR											

WORKOUT TRACKER

EXERCISE/ MUSCLES

BACK CHEST BICEPS TRICEPS FRONT DELTS REAR DELTS SIDE DELTS QUADS HAMSTRINGS GLUTES CALVES TRAPS ABS

DATE

START TIME

END TIME

CAD = Cadence

S = Set

WT = Weight

REPS = Repetitions

RIR = Repetitions In reserve

	CAD	S1	S2	S3	S4	S5	S6
WT							
REPS							
RIR							
WT							
REPS							
RIR							
WT							
REPS							
RIR							
WT							
REPS							
RIR							
WT							
REPS							
RIR							
WT							
REPS							
RIR							
WT							
REPS							
RIR							
WT							
REPS							
RIR							

REST REST REST REST REST

WORKOUT TRACKER

DATE

START TIME

END TIME

EXERCISE/ MUSCLES	CAD	S1	S2	S3	S4	S5	S6
	WT						
	REPS	REST	REST	REST	REST	REST	
	RIR						
	WT						
	REPS	REST	REST	REST	REST	REST	
	RIR						
	WT						
	REPS	REST	REST	REST	REST	REST	
	RIR						
	WT						
	REPS	REST	REST	REST	REST	REST	
	RIR						
	WT						
	REPS	REST	REST	REST	REST	REST	
	RIR						
	WT						
	REPS	REST	REST	REST	REST	REST	
	RIR						
	WT						
	REPS	REST	REST	REST	REST	REST	
	RIR						
	WT						
	REPS	REST	REST	REST	REST	REST	
	RIR						

BACK CHEST BICEPS TRICEPS FRONT DELTS REAR DELTS SIDE DELTS QUADS HAMSTRINGS GLUTES CALVES TRAPS ABS

CAD = Cadence

S = Set

WT = Weight

REPS = Repetitions

RIR = Repetitions In Reserve

© ULTIMATE **TRAINING** PLANNER

WORKOUT TRACKER

EXERCISE/ MUSCLES

BACK CHEST BICEPS TRICEPS FRONT DELTS REAR DELTS SIDE DELTS QUADS HAMSTRINGS GLUTES CALVES TRAPS ABS

DATE

START TIME

END TIME

EXERCISE/MUSCLES	CAD		S1		S2		S3		S4		S5		S6
		WT											
		REPS											
		RIR		REST		REST		REST		REST		REST	
		WT											
		REPS											
		RIR		REST		REST		REST		REST		REST	
		WT											
		REPS											
		RIR		REST		REST		REST		REST		REST	
		WT											
		REPS											
		RIR		REST		REST		REST		REST		REST	
		WT											
		REPS											
		RIR		REST		REST		REST		REST		REST	
		WT											
		REPS											
		RIR		REST		REST		REST		REST		REST	

CAD = Cadence **REPS** = Repetitions

S = Set **RIR** = Repetitions In Reserve

WT = Weight

WORKOUT TRACKER

DATE

START TIME

END TIME

CAD = Cadence
S = Set
WT = Weight

REPS = Repetitions
RIR = Repetitions in reserve

EXERCISE/ MUSCLES	BACK CHEST BICEPS TRICEPS FRONT DELTS REAR DELTS SIDE DELTS QUADS HAMSTRINGS GLUTES CALVES TRAPS ABS	CAD		S1	S2	S3	S4	S5	S6
			WT						
			REPS	REST	REST	REST	REST	REST	REST
			RIR						
			WT						
			REPS	REST	REST	REST	REST	REST	REST
			RIR						
			WT						
			REPS	REST	REST	REST	REST	REST	REST
			RIR						
			WT						
			REPS	REST	REST	REST	REST	REST	REST
			RIR						
			WT						
			REPS	REST	REST	REST	REST	REST	REST
			RIR						
			WT						
			REPS	REST	REST	REST	REST	REST	REST
			RIR						
			WT						
			REPS	REST	REST	REST	REST	REST	REST
			RIR						
			WT						
			REPS	REST	REST	REST	REST	REST	REST
			RIR						

WORKOUT TRACKER

DATE

START TIME

END TIME

CAD = Cadence
S = Set
WT = Weight
REPS = Repetitions
RIR = Repetitions in reserve

BACK CHEST BICEPS TRICEPS FRONT DELTS REAR DELTS SIDE DELTS QUADS HAMSTRINGS GLUTES CALVES TRAPS ABS

EXERCISE/ MUSCLES	CAD		S1	S2	S3	S4	S5	S6
		WT						
		REPS						
		RIR						
		WT						
		REPS						
		RIR						
		WT						
		REPS						
		RIR						
		WT						
		REPS						
		RIR						
		WT						
		REPS						
		RIR						
		WT						
		REPS						
		RIR						
		WT						
		REPS						
		RIR						
		WT						
		REPS						
		RIR						
		WT						
		REPS						
		RIR						
		WT						
		REPS						
		RIR						

WORKOUT TRACKER

EXERCISE/ MUSCLES

BACK CHEST BICEPS TRICEPS FRONT DELTS REAR DELTS SIDE DELTS QUADS HAMSTRINGS GLUTES CALVES TRAPS ABS

DATE

START TIME

END TIME

	CAD	S1	S2	S3	S4	S5	S6
WT / REPS / RIR			REST	REST	REST	REST	REST
WT / REPS / RIR			REST	REST	REST	REST	REST
WT / REPS / RIR			REST	REST	REST	REST	REST
WT / REPS / RIR			REST	REST	REST	REST	REST
WT / REPS / RIR			REST	REST	REST	REST	REST
WT / REPS / RIR			REST	REST	REST	REST	REST
WT / REPS / RIR			REST	REST	REST	REST	REST
WT / REPS / RIR			REST	REST	REST	REST	REST

CAD = Cadence
S = Set
WT = Weight
REPS = Repetitions
RIR = Repetitions in reserve

© ULTIMATE **TRAINING** PLANNER

WORKOUT TRACKER

EXERCISE/MUSCLES

BACK CHEST BICEPS TRICEPS FRONT DELTS REAR DELTS SIDE DELTS QUADS HAMSTRINGS GLUTES CALVES TRAPS ABS

DATE

START TIME

END TIME

CAD | S1 | S2 | S3 | S4 | S5 | S6

WT
REPS
RIR

REST

CAD = Cadence
S = Set
WT = Weight
REPS = Repetitions
RIR = Repetitions In reserve

WORKOUT TRACKER

EXERCISE/ MUSCLES

BACK CHEST BICEPS TRICEPS FRONT DELTS REAR DELTS SIDE DELTS QUADS HAMSTRINGS GLUTES CALVES TRAPS ABS

DATE

START TIME

END TIME

CAD	S1	S2	S3	S4	S5	S6
WT / REPS / RIR	REST	REST	REST	REST	REST	

CAD = Cadence

S = Set

WT = Weight

REPS = Repetitions

RIR = Repetitions in reserve

NUTRITION TRACKER

NUTRITION TRACKER

	CALORIES	PROTEIN	FAT	CARBS
MON				
TUE				
WED				
THU				
FRI				
SAT				
SUN				
AVERAGE Ø				
LAST WEEK Ø				

CALORIES

DATE

NUTRITION TRACKER

	CALORIES	PROTEIN	FAT	CARBS
MON				
TUE				
WED				
THU				
FRI				
SAT				
SUN				
AVERAGE Ø				
LAST WEEK Ø				

CALORIES

DATE

NUTRITION TRACKER

	CALORIES	PROTEIN	FAT	CARBS
MON				
TUE				
WED				
THU				
FRI				
SAT				
SUN				
AVERAGE Ø				
LAST WEEK Ø				

CALORIES

DATE

NUTRITION TRACKER

	CALORIES	PROTEIN	FAT	CARBS
MON				
TUE				
WED				
THU				
FRI				
SAT				
SUN				
AVERAGE Ø				
LAST WEEK Ø				

CALORIES

DATE

NUTRITION TRACKER

	CALORIES	PROTEIN	FAT	CARBS
MON				
TUE				
WED				
THU				
FRI				
SAT				
SUN				
AVERAGE Ø				
LAST WEEK Ø				

CALORIES

DATE

NUTRITION TRACKER

	CALORIES	PROTEIN	FAT	CARBS
MON				
TUE				
WED				
THU				
FRI				
SAT				
SUN				
AVERAGE Ø				
LAST WEEK Ø				

CALORIES

DATE

NUTRITION TRACKER

	CALORIES	PROTEIN	FAT	CARBS
MON				
TUE				
WED				
THU				
FRI				
SAT				
SUN				
AVERAGE Ø				
LAST WEEK Ø				

CALORIES

DATE

NUTRITION TRACKER

	CALORIES	PROTEIN	FAT	CARBS
MON				
TUE				
WED				
THU				
FRI				
SAT				
SUN				
AVERAGE Ø				
LAST WEEK Ø				

CALORIES

DATE

NUTRITION TRACKER

	CALORIES	PROTEIN	FAT	CARBS
MON				
TUE				
WED				
THU				
FRI				
SAT				
SUN				
AVERAGE Ø				
LAST WEEK Ø				

CALORIES

DATE

NUTRITION TRACKER

	CALORIES	PROTEIN	FAT	CARBS
MON				
TUE				
WED				
THU				
FRI				
SAT				
SUN				
AVERAGE Ø				
LAST WEEK Ø				

CALORIES

DATE

NUTRITION TRACKER

	CALORIES	PROTEIN	FAT	CARBS
MON				
TUE				
WED				
THU				
FRI				
SAT				
SUN				
AVERAGE Ø				
LAST WEEK Ø				

CALORIES

DATE

NUTRITION TRACKER

	CALORIES	PROTEIN	FAT	CARBS
MON				
TUE				
WED				
THU				
FRI				
SAT				
SUN				
AVERAGE Ø				
LAST WEEK Ø				

CALORIES

DATE

NUTRITION TRACKER

	CALORIES	PROTEIN	FAT	CARBS
MON				
TUE				
WED				
THU				
FRI				
SAT				
SUN				
AVERAGE Ø				
LAST WEEK Ø				

CALORIES

DATE

NUTRITION TRACKER

	CALORIES	PROTEIN	FAT	CARBS
MON				
TUE				
WED				
THU				
FRI				
SAT				
SUN				
AVERAGE Ø				
LAST WEEK Ø				

CALORIES

DATE

NUTRITION TRACKER

	CALORIES	PROTEIN	FAT	CARBS
MON				
TUE				
WED				
THU				
FRI				
SAT				
SUN				
AVERAGE Ø				
LAST WEEK Ø				

CALORIES

DATE

NUTRITION TRACKER

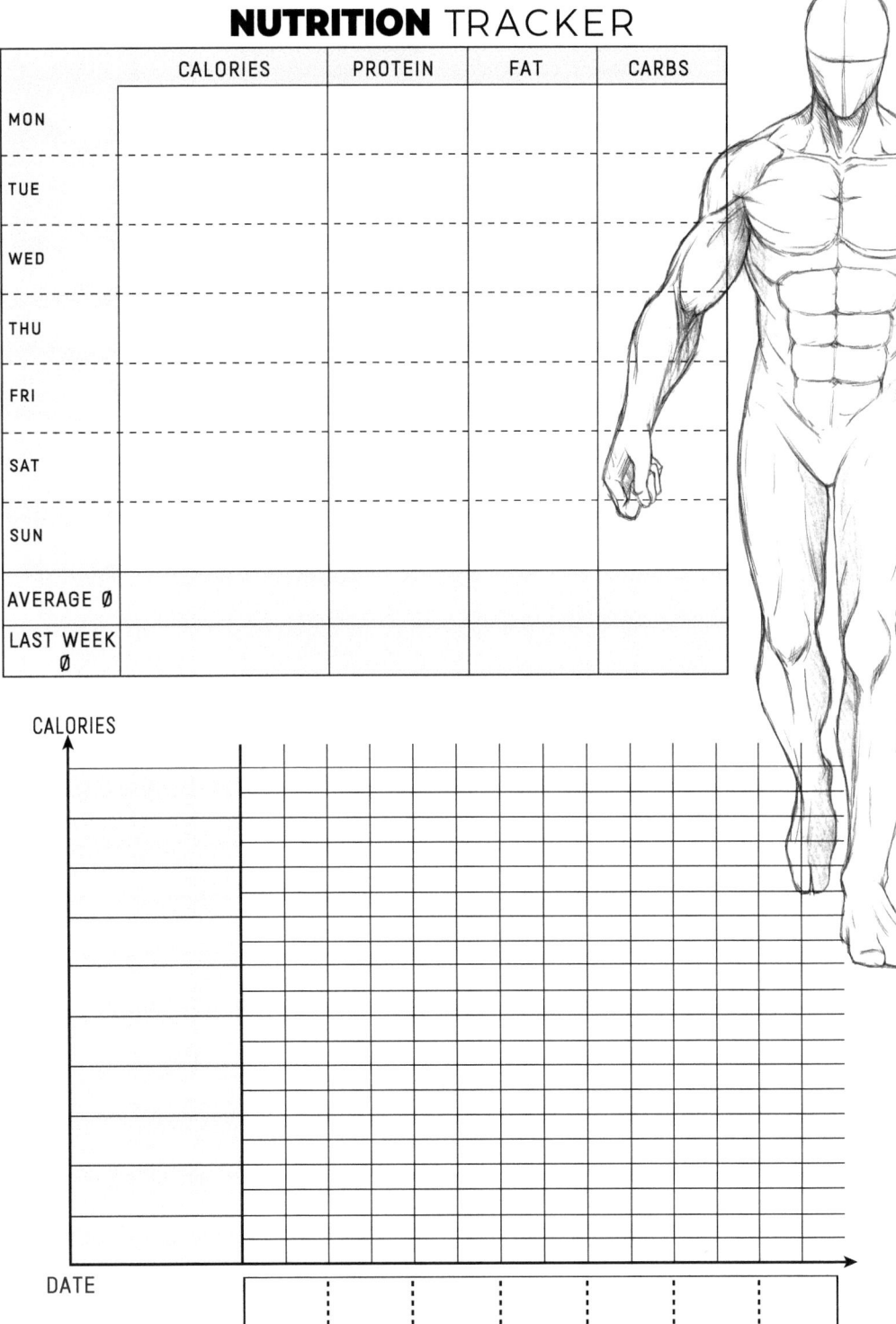

	CALORIES	PROTEIN	FAT	CARBS
MON				
TUE				
WED				
THU				
FRI				
SAT				
SUN				
AVERAGE Ø				
LAST WEEK Ø				

CALORIES

DATE

NUTRITION TRACKER

	CALORIES	PROTEIN	FAT	CARBS
MON				
TUE				
WED				
THU				
FRI				
SAT				
SUN				
AVERAGE Ø				
LAST WEEK Ø				

CALORIES

DATE

NUTRITION TRACKER

	CALORIES	PROTEIN	FAT	CARBS
MON				
TUE				
WED				
THU				
FRI				
SAT				
SUN				
AVERAGE Ø				
LAST WEEK Ø				

CALORIES

DATE

NUTRITION TRACKER

	CALORIES	PROTEIN	FAT	CARBS
MON				
TUE				
WED				
THU				
FRI				
SAT				
SUN				
AVERAGE Ø				
LAST WEEK Ø				

CALORIES

DATE

NUTRITION TRACKER

	CALORIES	PROTEIN	FAT	CARBS
MON				
TUE				
WED				
THU				
FRI				
SAT				
SUN				
AVERAGE Ø				
LAST WEEK Ø				

CALORIES

DATE

WEIGHT TRACKER

WEIGHT TRACKER

	WEIGHT	+/-	CALORIES	+/-
MON				
TUE				
WED				
THU				
FRI				
SAT				
SUN				
AVERAGE Ø				
LAST WEEK Ø				

WEIGHT

DATE

WEIGHT TRACKER

	WEIGHT	+/-	CALORIES	+/-
MON				
TUE				
WED				
THU				
FRI				
SAT				
SUN				
AVERAGE Ø				
LAST WEEK Ø				

WEIGHT

DATE

WEIGHT TRACKER

	WEIGHT	+/-	CALORIES	+/-
MON				
TUE				
WED				
THU				
FRI				
SAT				
SUN				
AVERAGE Ø				
LAST WEEK Ø				

WEIGHT

DATE

WEIGHT TRACKER

	WEIGHT	+/-	CALORIES	+/-
MON				
TUE				
WED				
THU				
FRI				
SAT				
SUN				
AVERAGE Ø				
LAST WEEK Ø				

WEIGHT

DATE

WEIGHT TRACKER

	WEIGHT	+/-	CALORIES	+/-
MON				
TUE				
WED				
THU				
FRI				
SAT				
SUN				
AVERAGE Ø				
LAST WEEK Ø				

WEIGHT

DATE

WEIGHT TRACKER

	WEIGHT	+/-	CALORIES	+/-
MON				
TUE				
WED				
THU				
FRI				
SAT				
SUN				
AVERAGE Ø				
LAST WEEK Ø				

WEIGHT

DATE

WEIGHT TRACKER

	WEIGHT	+/-	CALORIES	+/-
MON				
TUE				
WED				
THU				
FRI				
SAT				
SUN				
AVERAGE Ø				
LAST WEEK Ø				

WEIGHT

DATE

WEIGHT TRACKER

	WEIGHT	+/-	CALORIES	+/-
MON				
TUE				
WED				
THU				
FRI				
SAT				
SUN				
AVERAGE Ø				
LAST WEEK Ø				

WEIGHT

DATE

WEIGHT TRACKER

	WEIGHT	+/-	CALORIES	+/-
MON				
TUE				
WED				
THU				
FRI				
SAT				
SUN				
AVERAGE Ø				
LAST WEEK Ø				

WEIGHT

DATE

WEIGHT TRACKER

	WEIGHT	+/-	CALORIES	+/-
MON				
TUE				
WED				
THU				
FRI				
SAT				
SUN				
AVERAGE Ø				
LAST WEEK Ø				

WEIGHT

DATE

WEIGHT TRACKER

	WEIGHT	+/-	CALORIES	+/-
MON				
TUE				
WED				
THU				
FRI				
SAT				
SUN				
AVERAGE Ø				
LAST WEEK Ø				

WEIGHT

DATE

WEIGHT TRACKER

	WEIGHT	+/-	CALORIES	+/-
MON				
TUE				
WED				
THU				
FRI				
SAT				
SUN				
AVERAGE Ø				
LAST WEEK Ø				

WEIGHT

DATE

WEIGHT TRACKER

	WEIGHT	+/-	CALORIES	+/-
MON				
TUE				
WED				
THU				
FRI				
SAT				
SUN				
AVERAGE Ø				
LAST WEEK Ø				

WEIGHT

DATE

WEIGHT TRACKER

	WEIGHT	+/-	CALORIES	+/-
MON				
TUE				
WED				
THU				
FRI				
SAT				
SUN				
AVERAGE Ø				
LAST WEEK Ø				

WEIGHT

DATE

WEIGHT TRACKER

	WEIGHT	+/-	CALORIES	+/-
MON				
TUE				
WED				
THU				
FRI				
SAT				
SUN				
AVERAGE Ø				
LAST WEEK Ø				

WEIGHT

DATE

WEIGHT TRACKER

	WEIGHT	+/-	CALORIES	+/-
MON				
TUE				
WED				
THU				
FRI				
SAT				
SUN				
AVERAGE Ø				
LAST WEEK Ø				

WEIGHT

DATE

WEIGHT TRACKER

	WEIGHT	+/-	CALORIES	+/-
MON				
TUE				
WED				
THU				
FRI				
SAT				
SUN				
AVERAGE Ø				
LAST WEEK Ø				

WEIGHT

DATE

WEIGHT TRACKER

	WEIGHT	+/-	CALORIES	+/-
MON				
TUE				
WED				
THU				
FRI				
SAT				
SUN				
AVERAGE Ø				
LAST WEEK Ø				

WEIGHT

DATE

WEIGHT TRACKER

	WEIGHT	+/-	CALORIES	+/-
MON				
TUE				
WED				
THU				
FRI				
SAT				
SUN				
AVERAGE Ø				
LAST WEEK Ø				

WEIGHT

DATE

WEIGHT TRACKER

	WEIGHT	+/-	CALORIES	+/-
MON				
TUE				
WED				
THU				
FRI				
SAT				
SUN				
AVERAGE Ø				
LAST WEEK Ø				

WEIGHT

DATE

VOLUME TRACKER

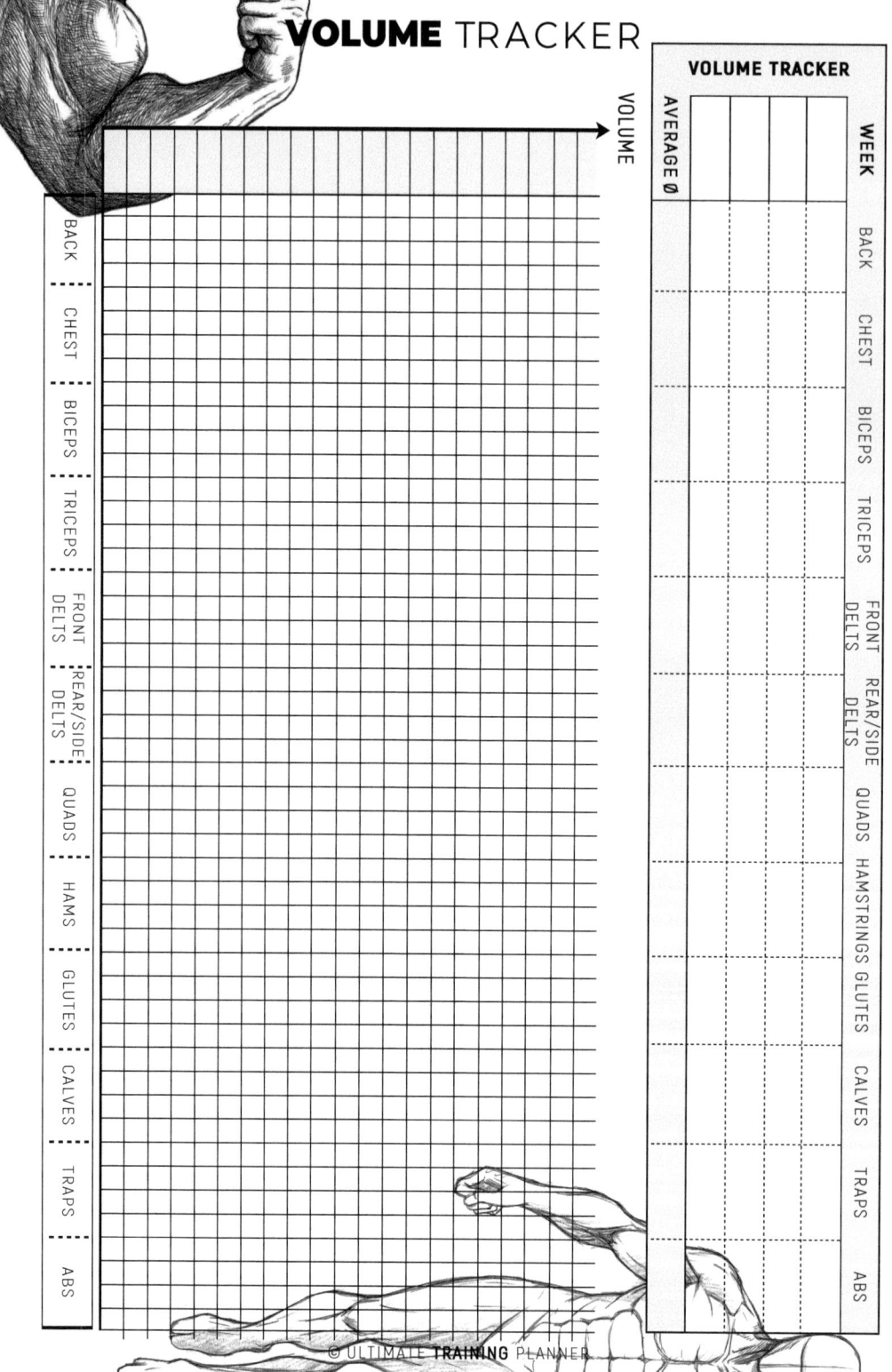

VOLUME TRACKER

VOLUME

BACK · · · · · CHEST · · · · · BICEPS · · · · · TRICEPS · · · · · FRONT DELTS · · · · · REAR/SIDE DELTS · · · · · QUADS · · · · · HAMS · · · · · GLUTES · · · · · CALVES · · · · · TRAPS · · · · · ABS

VOLUME TRACKER

WEEK	AVERAGE Ø			
BACK				
CHEST				
BICEPS				
TRICEPS				
FRONT DELTS				
REAR/SIDE DELTS				
QUADS				
HAMSTRINGS				
GLUTES				
CALVES				
TRAPS				
ABS				

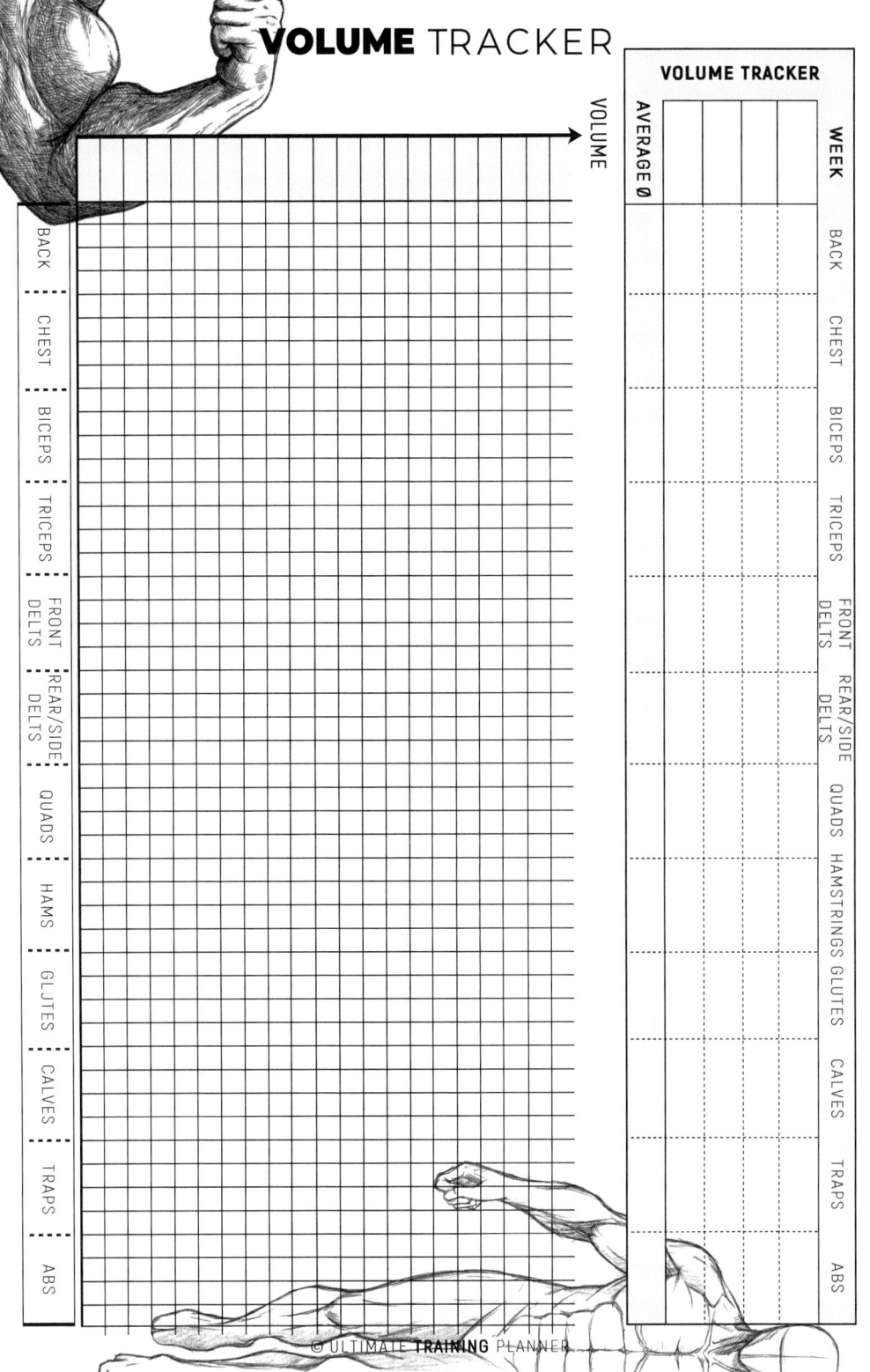

VOLUME TRACKER

VOLUME

BACK
CHEST
BICEPS
TRICEPS
FRONT DELTS
REAR/SIDE DELTS
QUADS
HAMS
GLUTES
CALVES
TRAPS
ABS

VOLUME TRACKER

WEEK				AVERAGE Ø
BACK				
CHEST				
BICEPS				
TRICEPS				
FRONT DELTS				
REAR/SIDE DELTS				
QUADS				
HAMSTRINGS GLUTES				
CALVES				
TRAPS				
ABS				

VOLUME TRACKER

VOLUME

BACK

CHEST

BICEPS

TRICEPS

FRONT DELTS

REAR/SIDE DELTS

QUADS

HAMS

GLUTES

CALVES

TRAPS

ABS

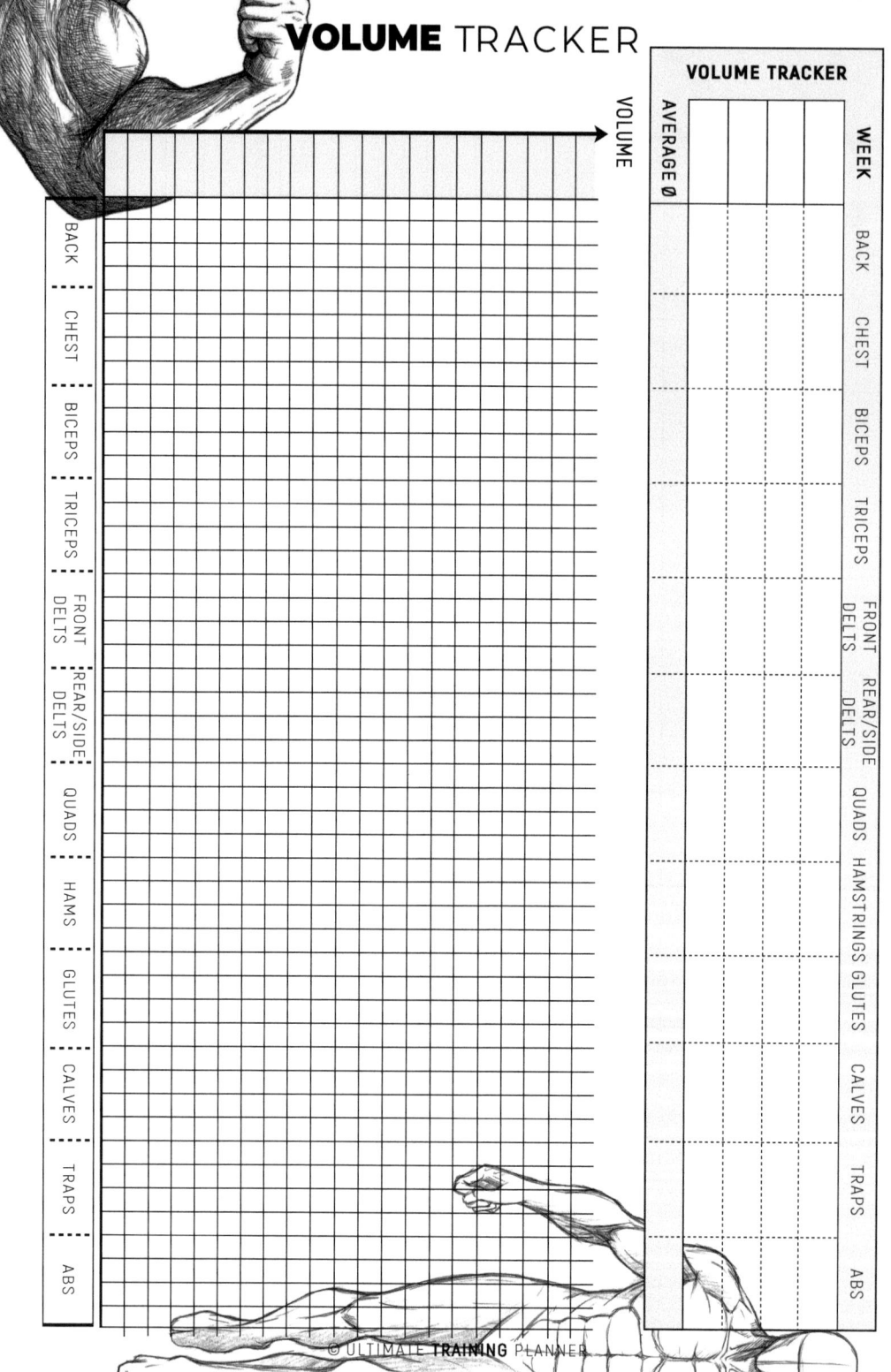

VOLUME TRACKER

WEEK	AVERAGE Ø				
BACK					
CHEST					
BICEPS					
TRICEPS					
FRONT DELTS					
REAR/SIDE DELTS					
QUADS					
HAMSTRINGS					
GLUTES					
CALVES					
TRAPS					
ABS					

VOLUME TRACKER

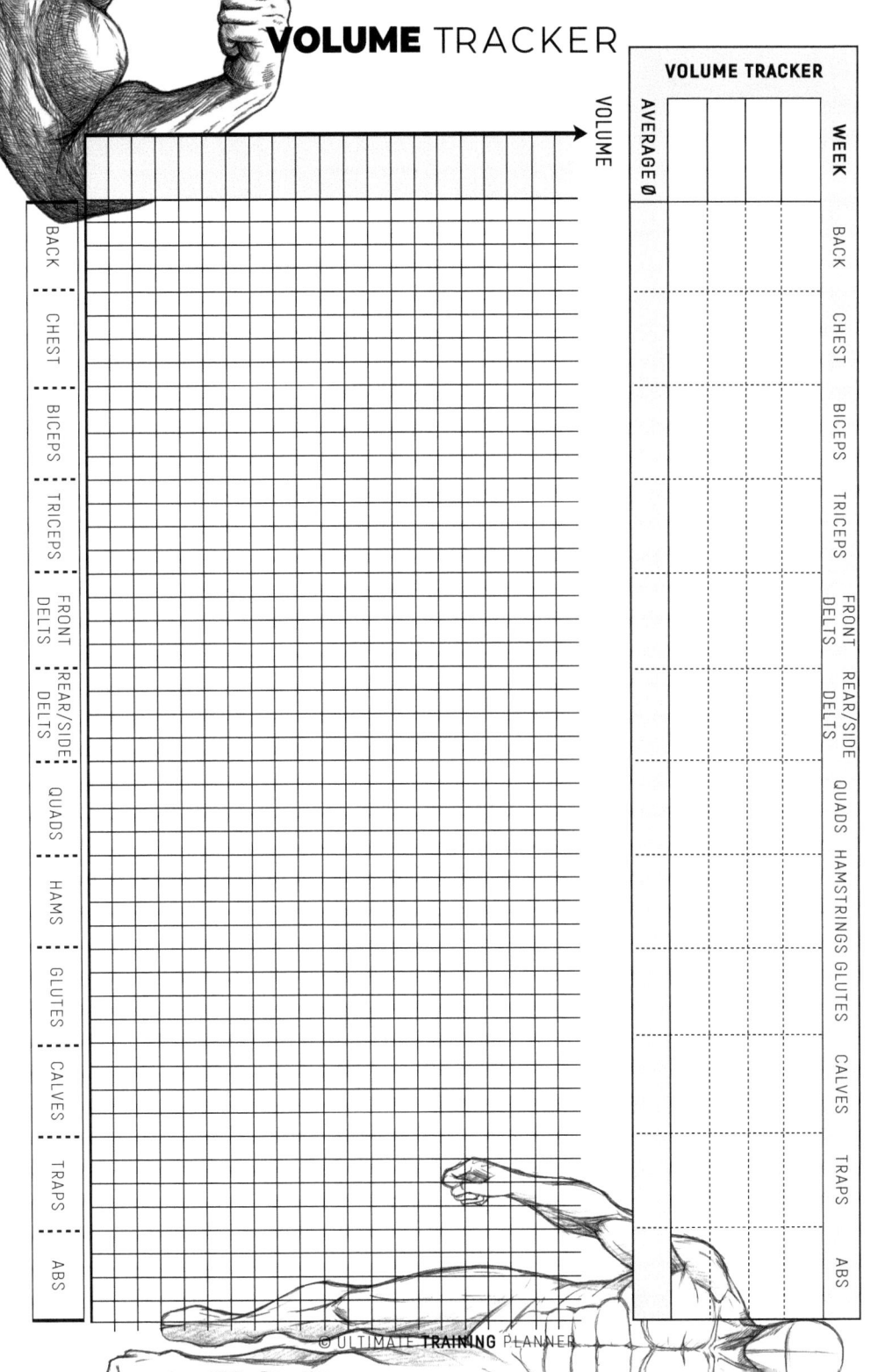

VOLUME

BACK
CHEST
BICEPS
TRICEPS
FRONT DELTS
REAR/SIDE DELTS
QUADS
HAMS
GLUTES
CALVES
TRAPS
ABS

VOLUME TRACKER

WEEK

AVERAGE Ø

BACK
CHEST
BICEPS
TRICEPS
FRONT DELTS
REAR/SIDE DELTS
QUADS
HAMSTRINGS
GLUTES
CALVES
TRAPS
ABS

© ULTIMATE TRAINING PLANNER

VOLUME TRACKER

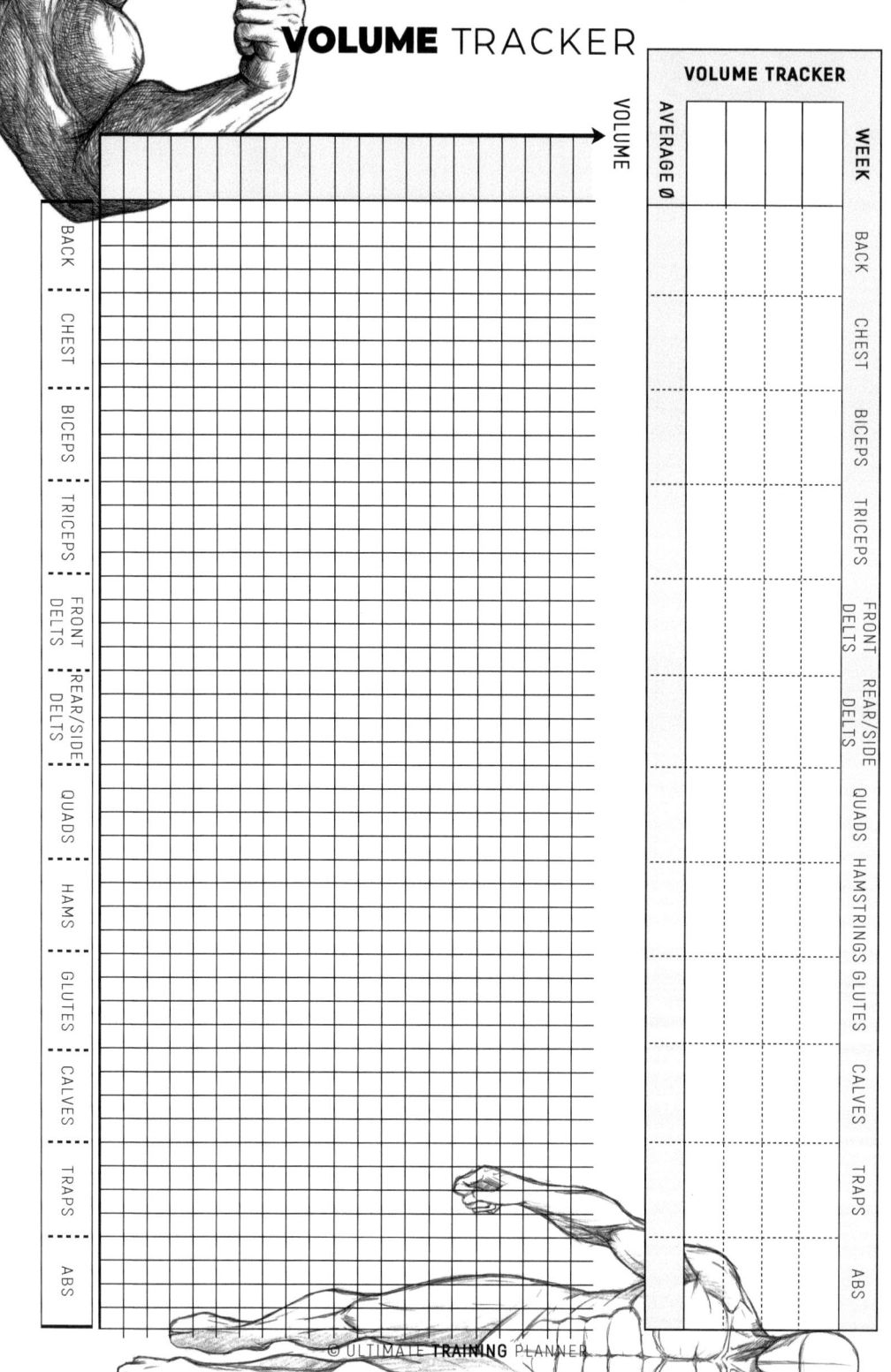

VOLUME

BACK · CHEST · BICEPS · TRICEPS · FRONT DELTS · REAR/SIDE DELTS · QUADS · HAMS · GLUTES · CALVES · TRAPS · ABS

VOLUME TRACKER

WEEK				
AVERAGE Ø				

BACK · CHEST · BICEPS · TRICEPS · FRONT DELTS · REAR/SIDE DELTS · QUADS · HAMSTRINGS · GLUTES · CALVES · TRAPS · ABS

MEASUREMENTS TRACKER

MEASUREMENTS TRACKER

DATE

BEFORE   AFTER   GOAL

9
8
7
6
5
4
2

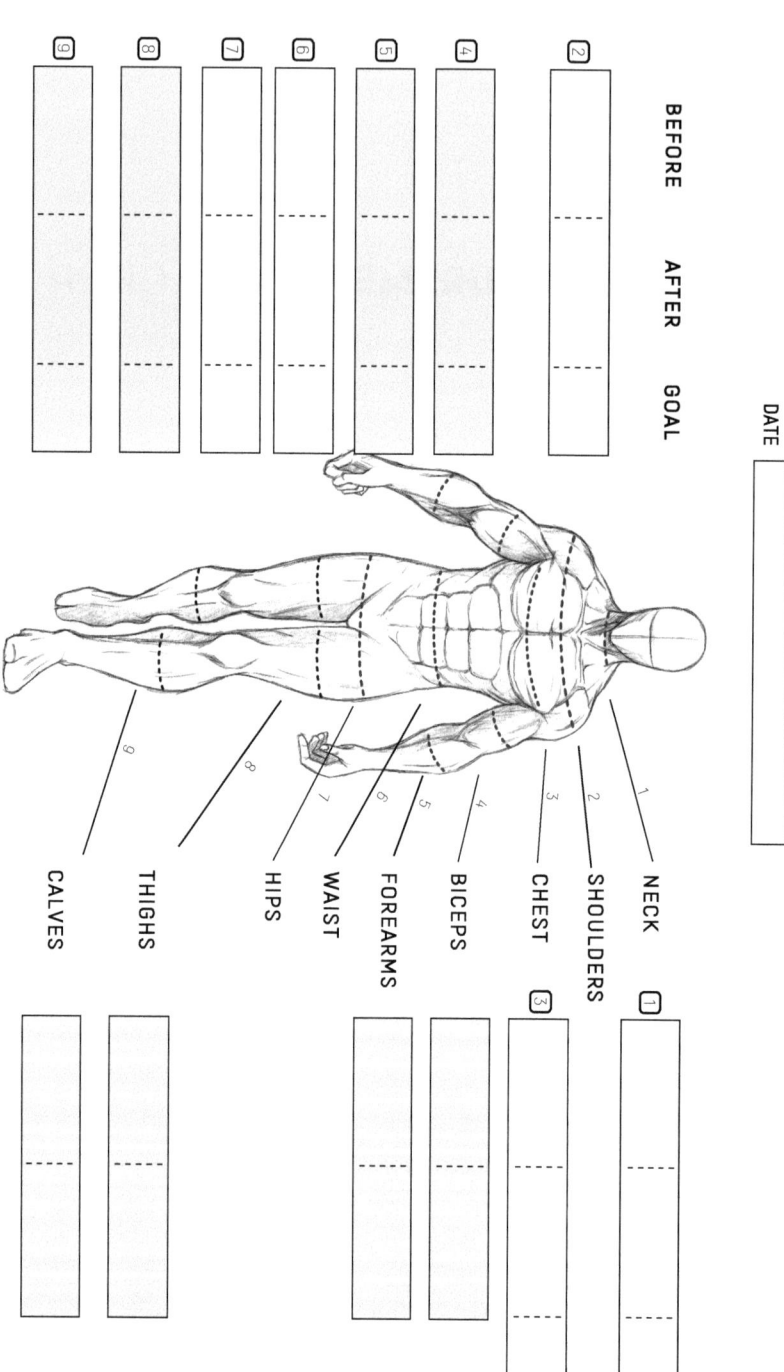

1 NECK
2 SHOULDERS
3 CHEST
4 BICEPS
5 FOREARMS
6 WAIST
7 HIPS
8 THIGHS
9 CALVES

3
1

MEASUREMENTS TRACKER

DATE

BEFORE   AFTER   GOAL

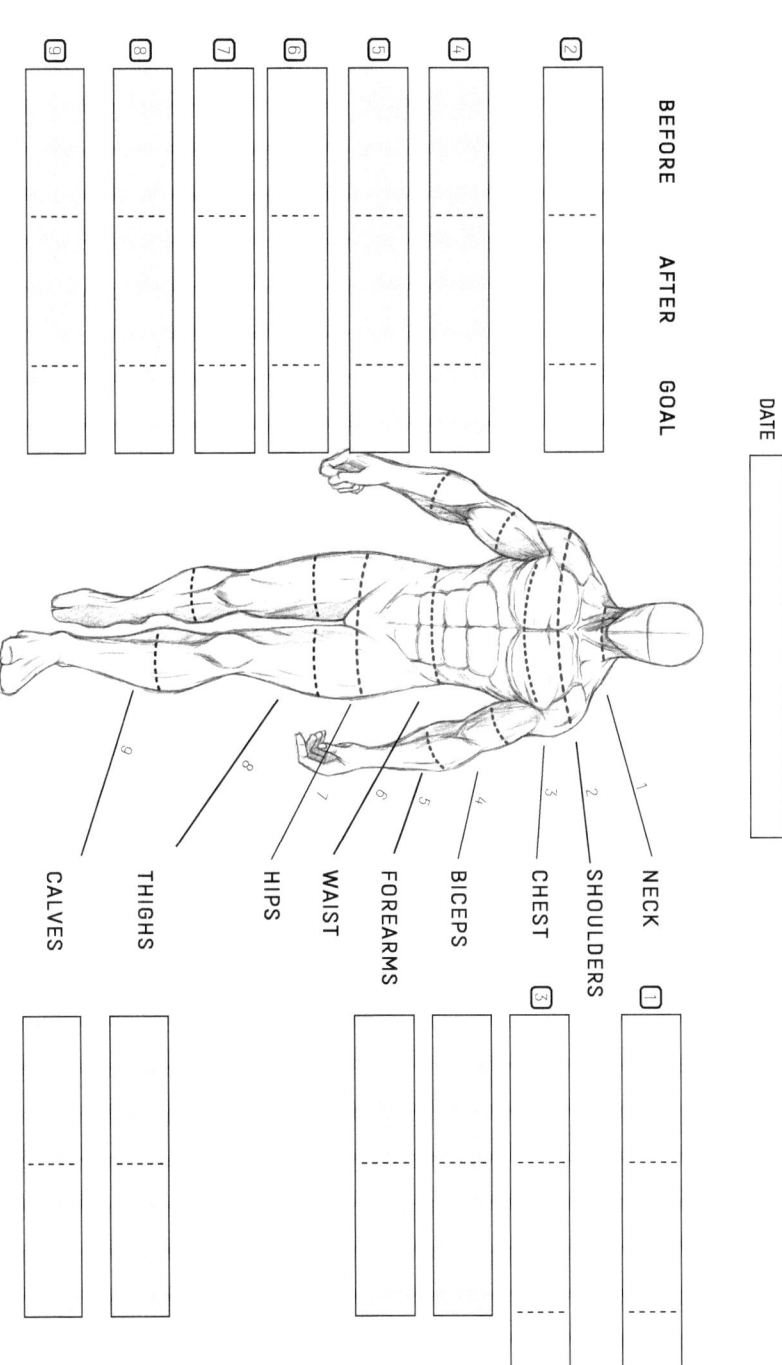

1. NECK
2. SHOULDERS
3. CHEST
4. BICEPS
5. FOREARMS
6. WAIST
7. HIPS
8. THIGHS
9. CALVES

MEASUREMENTS TRACKER

DATE

BEFORE   AFTER   GOAL

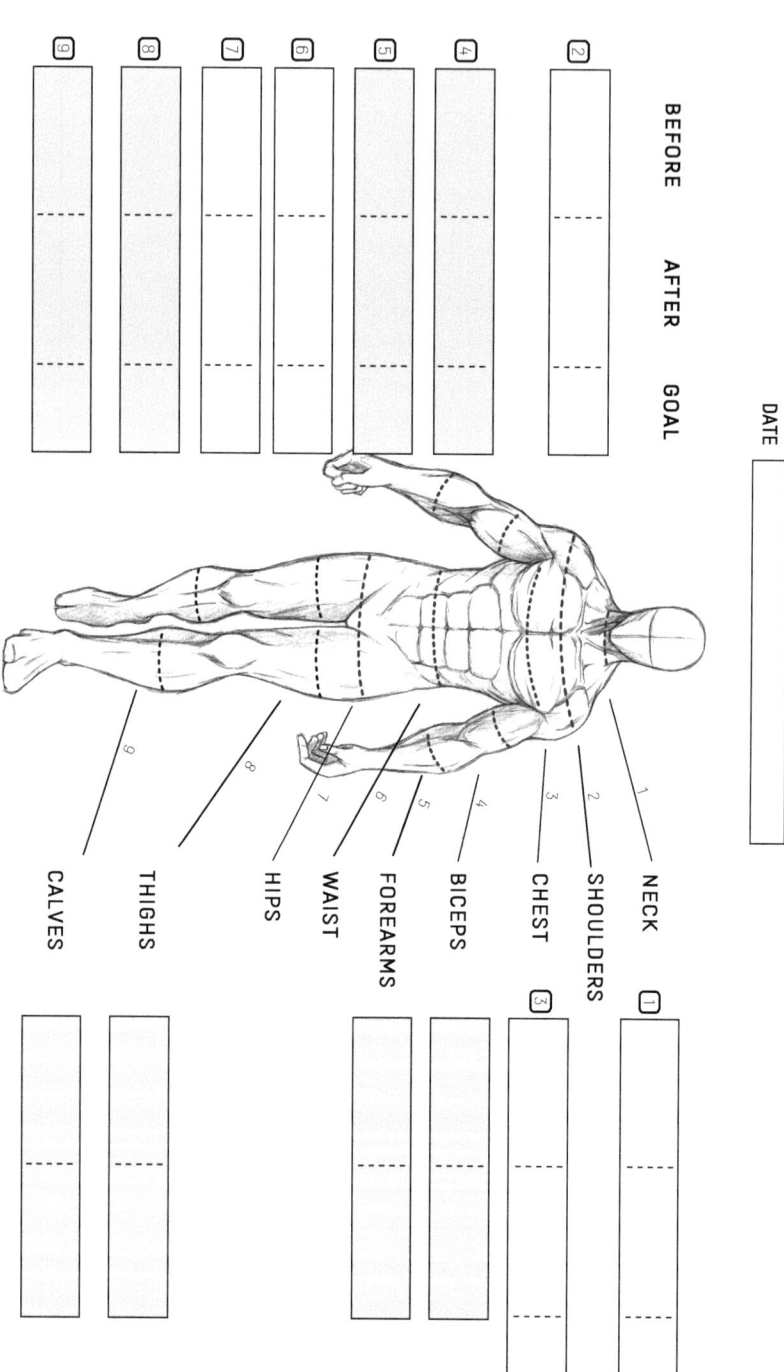

1 NECK
2 SHOULDERS
3 CHEST
4 BICEPS
5 FOREARMS
6 WAIST
7 HIPS
8 THIGHS
9 CALVES

MEASUREMENTS TRACKER

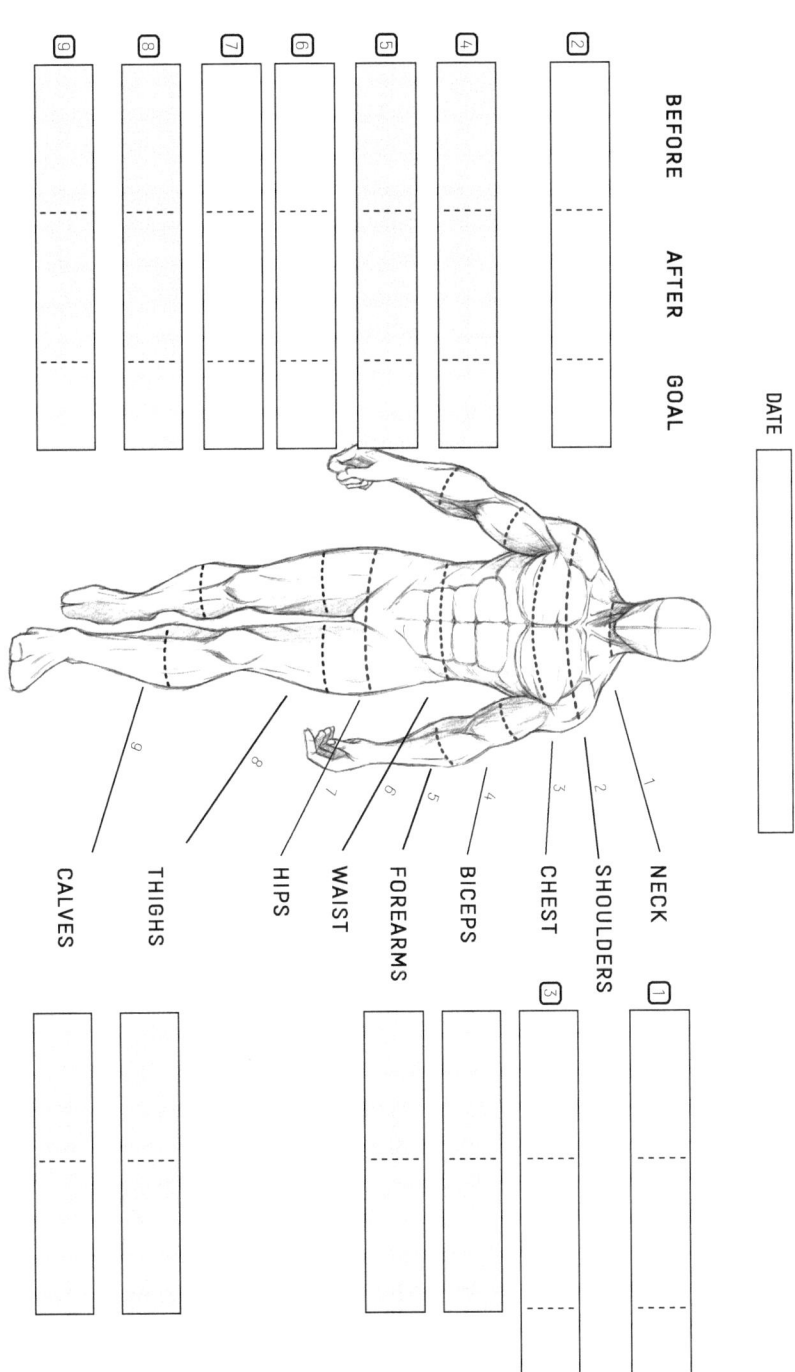

BEFORE   AFTER   GOAL

DATE

9
8
7
6
5
4
2
1
3

NECK
SHOULDERS
CHEST
BICEPS
FOREARMS
WAIST
HIPS
THIGHS
CALVES

MEASUREMENTS TRACKER

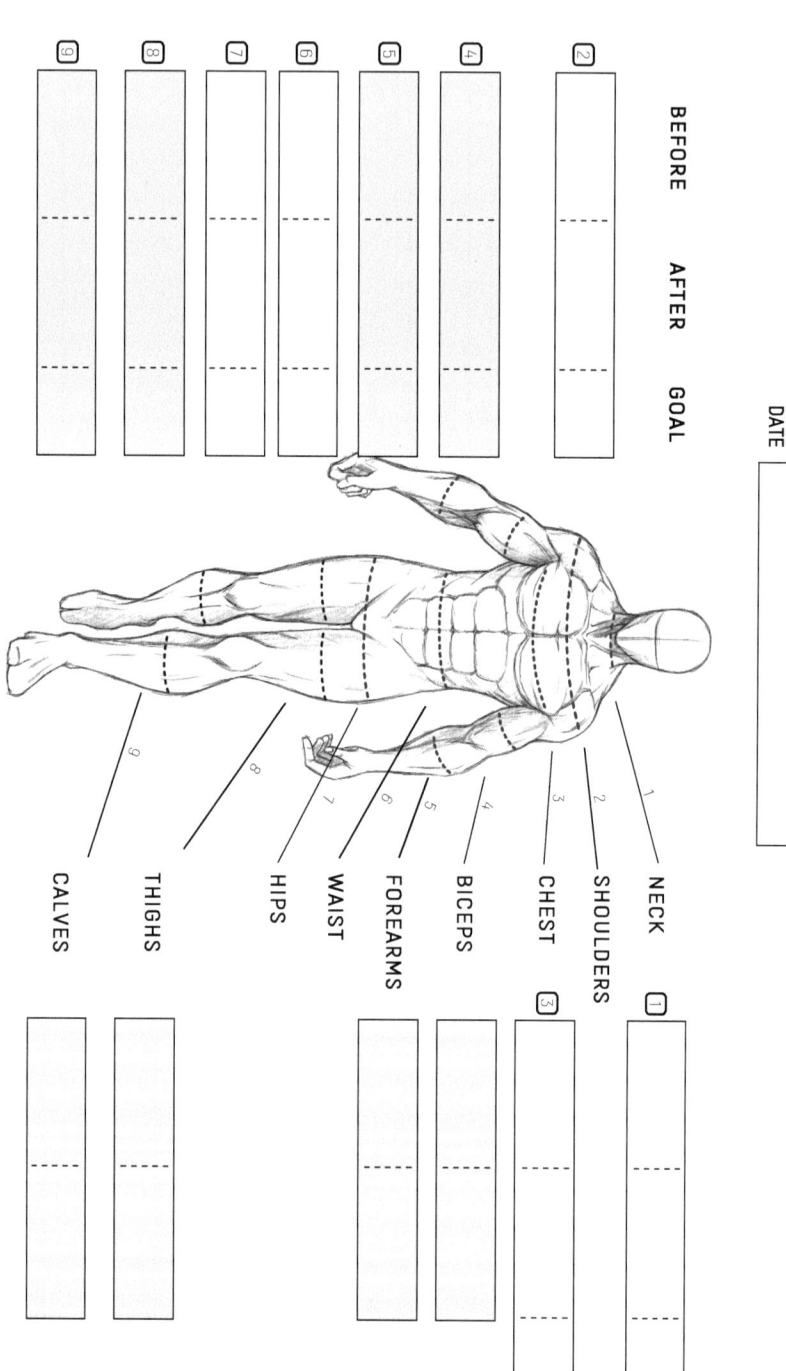

BEFORE   AFTER   GOAL

DATE

NECK
SHOULDERS
CHEST
BICEPS
FOREARMS
WAIST
HIPS
THIGHS
CALVES